SINGER SIMPLE

mending and repair

essential machine-side tips and techniques

the editors of SINGER Worldwide

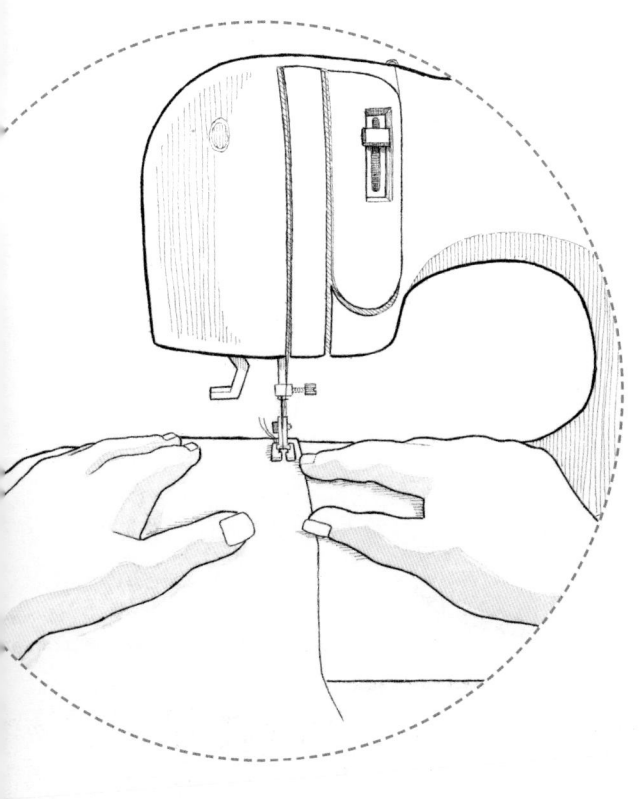

Creative Publishing international

Copyright © 2007
Creative Publishing international, Inc.
18705 Lake Drive East
Chanhassen, Minnesota 55317
1-800-328-3895
www.creativepub.com

ISBN–13: 978-1-58923-340-9
ISBN–10: 1-58923-340-9

10 9 8 7 6 5 4 3 2 1

Library of Congress Cataloging-in-Publication Data

Singer simple mending & repair : essential machine-side tips and techniques / the editors of Singer worldwide.
        p. cm.
    Includes index.

    1. Machine sewing. 2. Clothing and dress--Repairing. I. Singer Sewing Machine Company. II. Title.

    TT713.S55 2007

    646.2'04--dc22

                                                    2007024201
                                                    CIP

Author: Beth Baumgartel

Tech Editor: Carol Fresia

Page Layout: Susan Gilday

Illustrator: Heather Lambert

Printed in China

contents

fix it yourself!
Here's what you need to know

Even if you've never threaded a needle, you can mend a favorite shirt, repair a broken zipper, fix a torn cushion, or shorten a pair of pants. It's easy with *Singer Simple Mending and Repair,* a comprehensive guide to fixing clothing, outdoor gear, and home décor.

You'll be surprised to see how much money you can save. You'll also learn how to save your favorite clothes and accessories. So before you throw anything away, think again! You can just fix it!

Whether you've never picked up a needle, or are a sometimes sewer, clothing repair is an easy skill to learn and a handy one to have. Mending not only gives you a great feeling of satisfaction, it saves you a trip to the tailor or to the store to hunt for a replacement item. Nobody seems to darn socks anymore, but why not? All it takes is a needle and thread—and you can keep wearing those great socks (at least until one goes missing in the wash).

You don't even need a sewing machine.

Armed with just a few basic sewing tools, you can learn to fix a tear, patch a hole, replace a button, repair a hem, and remove a stain. A sewing machine is great for some types of repairs, but nearly every kind of mending job can also be done by hand. *Singer Simple Mending and Repair* is the must-have, how-to book for the care and repair of your favorite things!

assessing the damage

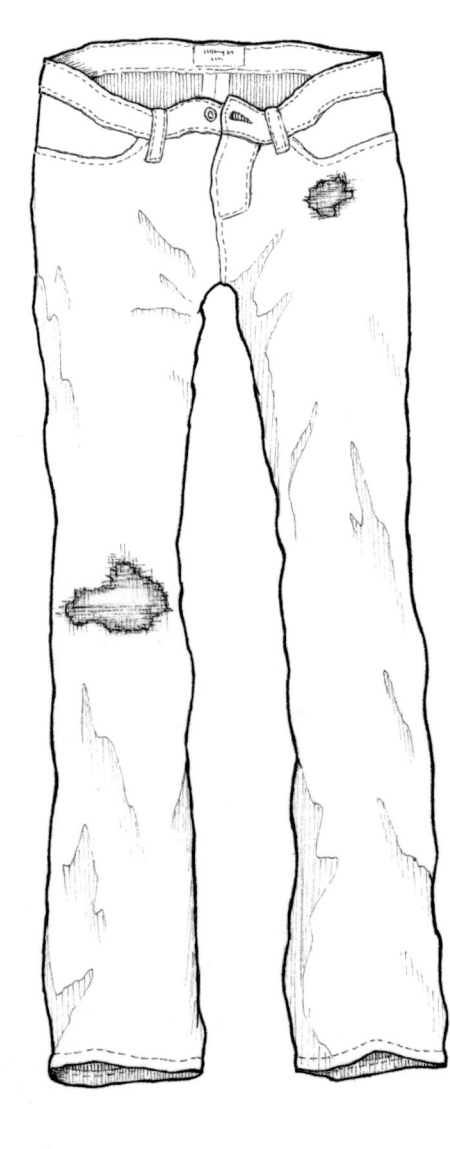

Mending is a simple job. You don't have to be an experienced sewer, but you do have to decide whether the item is actually able to be fixed—and whether your time is worth the effort.

Examine the damaged area. Trim away loose threads to neaten the hole or tear. Try to catch rips and holes before they get too large—the larger the damaged area, the harder it is to fix inconspicuously. Reinforce frayed or thinning fabric before it tears, and take action against stains, spots, and scorch marks as soon as possible.

You can make simple repair jobs (fixing torn hems and ripped seams) while you watch television. Other jobs (replacing a zipper or darning a hole) require a bit more attention. But if the garment in need of repair is your favorite jacket or your most comfortable pants, it just might be worth it.

What's It Worth?

Consider whether the repair will be visible, whether the item will still fit after it's repaired (sometimes you have to sacrifice space in a garment to fix a tear), and whether it might just take less time and effort to replace it. You can easily patch a tear in the knee of a pair of jeans, but making an invisible repair in a fine knit, for example, is a little more challenging.

Expensive clothing, draperies, and cushions are usually made of good quality fabric—which, fortunately, is easier to repair than cheaper fabric. If the item is expensive, one of your favorites, or an heirloom, definitely try to repair it. Even if you are okay with giving the item away—to charity or as a hand-me-down—why not try to fix it first? You have nothing to lose—and the person on the receiving end will appreciate the effort!

checklist of considerations

Simple mending gives almost everything new life. If the damage seems beyond your skill level, take the garment to a tailor. But remember, you'll rarely do more damage if you give the repair a try yourself first.

✓ Is the fabric of good quality?

✓ Is it easy to find a replacement item?

✓ Is the item expensive to replace?

✓ Is the item part of a set or an outfit?

✓ Is the item a favorite, with sentimental value?

✓ Is the fabric easy to work with?

✓ Is the damage in a visible or central area?

✓ How large is the damaged area?

✓ Is the rest of the garment or item still in good shape?

✓ Is the fabric frayed around the damaged area?

✓ Is the fabric stretched out of shape?

✓ Is the area around the tear stretched or distorted?

✓ Will the color and/or design be hard to match?

✓ Will a patch or repair stitching be unsightly?

✓ Can you make a decorative repair?

✓ Are you nervous about taking on this kind of repair?

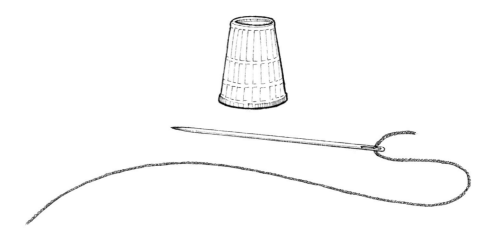

common repairs

Some mending and repair projects are easy. If a button falls off your jacket, just sew it back on before you leave the house—it's that easy. Other types of repairs, such as mending a torn buttonhole, aren't difficult—they just take a little longer to complete. Here are some of the most common mending projects, listed by degree of difficulty. The biggest factors in complexity are the location of the damage, the type of fabric, and the techniques required to make the repair.

Easiest Repair Projects

Fabrics: fleece, fake fur, moderate to heavyweight knits, patterned and textured fabrics

- Fixing a torn hem
- Shortening any type of garment
- Darning a hole in an unobtrusive location or on sport/casual work clothes
- Darning a hole in knit, fleece, or pile fabrics
- Patching play clothes and casual clothing
- Fixing a ripped seam
- Mending an inseam pocket
- Sewing on a button
- Fixing a partially ripped buttonhole
- Restitching a partially ripped but working zipper
- Replacing elastic in a casing
- Darning a snag or a pulled thread
- Taking in clothing at the seams
- Repairing topstitching
- Restringing a drawstring

More Challenging Projects

Fabrics: broadcloth, denim, machine-made lace, single knits, solid-color fabrics

- Lengthening any type of garment
- Adding a cuff to pants
- Adding a ruffle to the bottom edge of any item
- Darning a hole in an obvious location on everyday clothing
- Darning a hole in flat, woven fabrics
- Re-attaching a torn patch pocket
- Repairing a fabric tear under a button
- Fixing a frayed or substantially ripped buttonhole
- Repairing ripped lining
- Reshaping clothing at the seams
- Fixing a dart or vent that has ripped open
- Replacing stitched-on elastic
- Removing some types of stains

Most Challenging Projects

Fabrics: lace, leather, satin, silk, velvet

- Darning a hole in satin weave and shiny eveningwear fabrics
- Darning invisibly in a conspicuous location
- Fixing a rip in the center (not the seam) of a garment
- Repairing specialty fabrics, such as lace, metallics, sequined fabrics, and leather
- Stabilizing a stretched buttonhole and fixing a completely ripped buttonhole
- Replacing a broken zipper
- Replacing lining
- Darning burn holes
- Letting out clothing
- Removing some types of stains, water marks, or pressing shine

notions

Keep a basic supply of these helpful items on hand and store them in a pretty basket or box. If you have to run to the store every time you need to mend something, the repair probably won't ever get done!

thread: All-purpose thread is all you need for most repairs, including resewing seams, patching, and replacing closures. Buttonhole twist or other heavy-duty thread is handy for attaching buttons on heavy fabrics.

Purchase thread in black, white, and a few other basic colors, such as navy, khaki, and mid-tone gray—these will blend with nearly any fabric color.

fasteners: Look for snaps and hooks and eyes in assorted sizes.

buttons: Keep a supply of white and black flat buttons in a variety of sizes.

seam tape: Basic white and black seam tape is great for quick fixes.

fusible interfacing, web, and stabilizer: Buy 1/4 yard (22.8 cm), for quick patching and stabilizing.

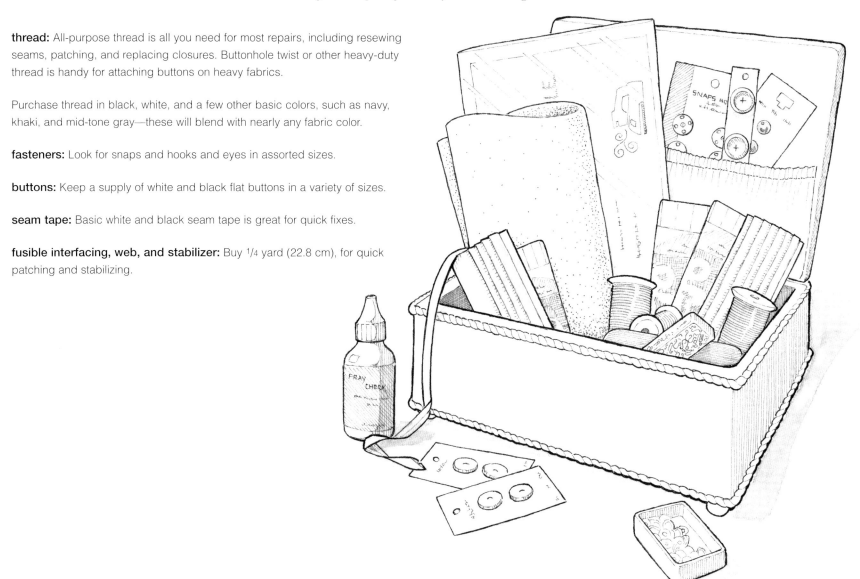

tools

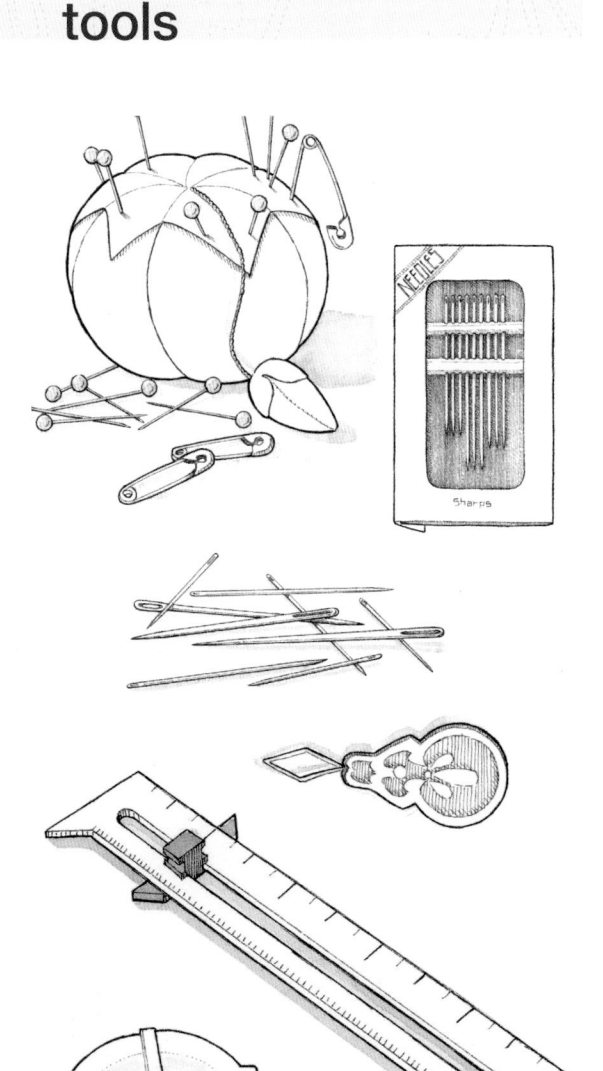

There's no need for a lot of sewing gadgets. A few basics will help you get the job done. Many mending projects are done by hand, so keep a small supply of sewing tools handy.

straight pins, safety pins, and a pin cushion: Keep a supply of dressmaker straight pins and safety pins. To prevent spills and keep them handy, store them in a pin cushion or on a magnetic pin-holder.

hand-sewing needles: Sharps are all-purpose, medium-length needles with sharp points for seaming and general hand sewing.

darning needles: Darning needles are very long with fine points for darning holes by hand.

needle threader: This small wire loop enables you to thread needles easily (see page 16).

thimble: Wear a thimble on the third finger of your sewing hand so you can push the needle through heavy fabrics without hurting your finger.

seam gauge: A seam gauge is great for taking small measurements, especially seam allowances and hems.

measuring tape: A flexible tape measure, 60" (152.4 cm) long, is soft but not stretchy. It is used for measuring the body and curved seams.

beeswax: Run your hand-sewing thread across a piece of beeswax to strengthen it and prevent it from fraying and tangling.

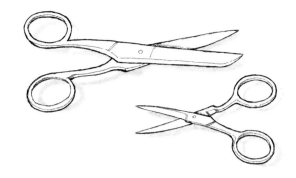

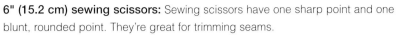
6" (15.2 cm) sewing scissors: Sewing scissors have one sharp point and one blunt, rounded point. They're great for trimming seams.

3" or 4" (7.6 or 10.1 cm) embroidery scissors: These small scissors with two sharp points are ideal for precision cutting and snipping thread ends.

seam ripper: With this precise, invaluable tool, you can remove unwanted stitches without ripping the fabric.

chalk wedge/pencil or fabric-marking pen: These tools will help you accurately copy design lines or mark alteration and new sewing lines.

steam iron, ironing board and press cloth (scrap of muslin or plain white cotton): When pressing repair areas, cover the item with a press cloth to protect the fabric from the iron, and the iron from any fusible adhesives that might be present.

liquid fray preventer: This liquid prevents fabric and trim from fraying. It is also used to secure thread ends. It is washable and dry-cleanable and does not discolor or stain most fabrics. (Test it first on an inconspicuous area.)

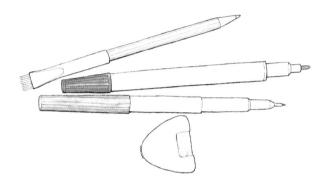

Remove unwanted liquid fray preventer by blotting the area with a cotton ball dipped in rubbing alcohol.

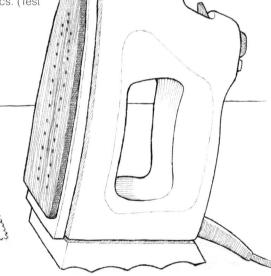

the sewing machine

For sturdy and quick repairs, you'll find a sewing machine invaluable. Zipper replacements, patches, and darns are stronger when machine-stitched (even though you can also work by hand).

All you need are straight and zigzag stitches, which are featured on even the most basic sewing machine. Refer to your owner's manual for specific operating instructions.

If you have never used a sewing machine, practice a few straight lines of stitching on scrap fabric, and you'll be ready to go. If you have any problem with skipped or uneven stitches, rethread the sewing machine and remove and reinsert the bobbin. Nine times out of ten, that will fix the problem. You might also replace the needle, because an old needle can cause irregular stitches.

Start every project with a new needle or change the needle after approximately eight hours of sewing.

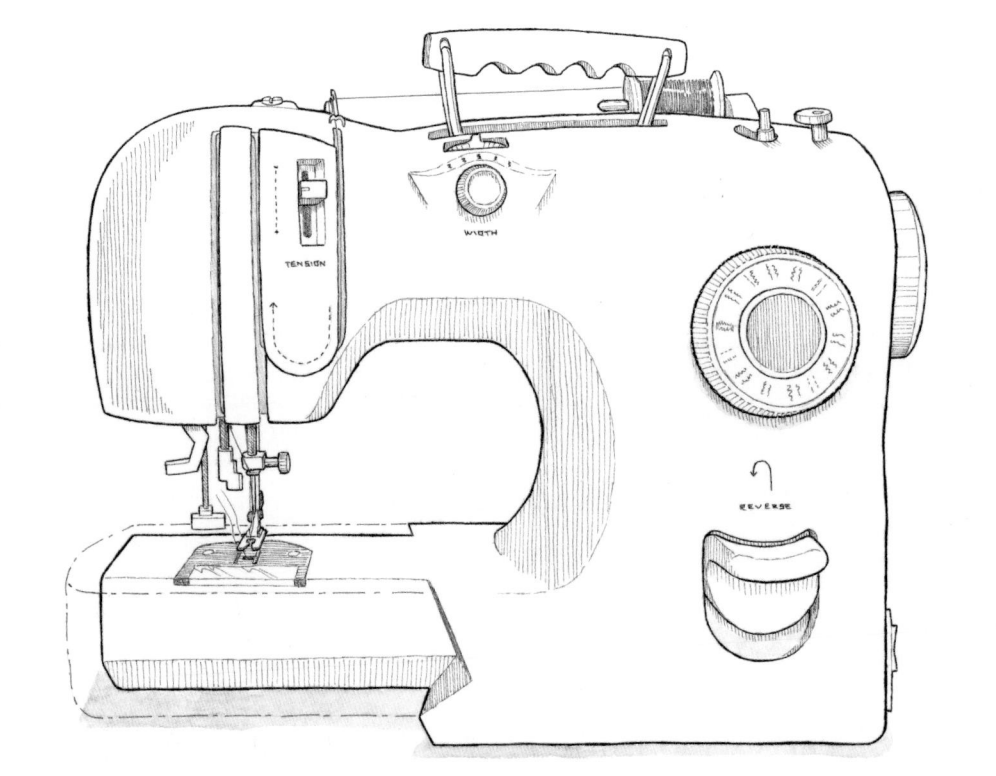

needles, bobbins, and presser feet

Set your machine up correctly for smooth sewing: choosing the right sewing machine accessories will help you make professional-looking repairs.

Needles

A sharp point needle is best for woven fabrics and a ballpoint needle for knits. The most widely used needle sizes are 12/80 and 14/90. The smaller numbers indicate thinner needles, necessary for lighter weight fabrics. Choose larger needles for heavier fabrics. A twin needle makes quick work of parallel topstitching.

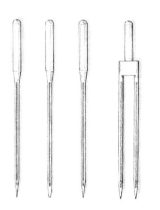

Bobbins

The machine's lower thread is wound around a metal or plastic bobbin that fits under the needle plate. Refer to your sewing machine manual to learn how to wind and insert a bobbin.

Presser Feet

The standard, all-purpose presser foot and the zipper foot that come with every sewing machine are suitable for most types of sewing. Additional feet, sometimes included with the machine but sold in most fabric stores, are designed to make specific sewing tasks easier.

all-purpose foot: This foot is perfect for all general sewing. Its wide needle opening is good for both straight and zigzag stitching.

zipper foot: This narrow foot helps you stitch close to a raised edge, and is ideal for replacing zippers and attaching piping, welting, and some trims.

blind hem foot: The blade on this foot serves as a guide along fabric folds or edges, for even, invisible machine hemming.

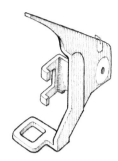

darning foot: This loop-shaped foot holds the fabric surface taut for machine darning and free-motion embroidery.

open-toe embroidery foot: The groove on the underside of this foot glides over raised decorative stitching, and the space between toes offers greater stitch visibility as you work.

general guidelines

Before you start mending anything, review these simple tips to make your job easier! Damaged areas will always get worse over time, so the sooner you repair them, the simpler the job will be.

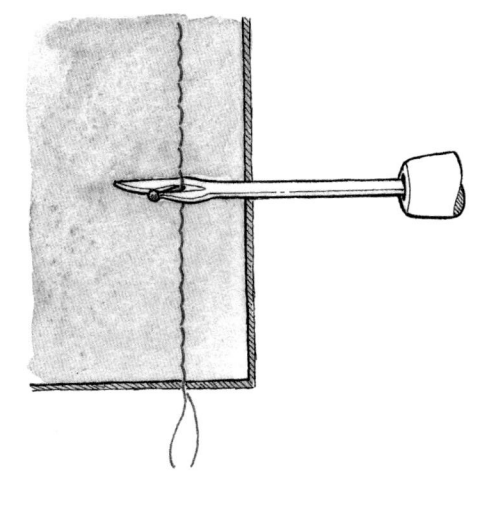

- Always work in good light.
- Press the repair area before you begin.
- Mend the item before you wash it, to prevent further fraying or tearing.
- Select a thread that matches the color of the item. If you can't find the exact shade of thread, choose one that is slightly darker than the fabric.

- Take action to avoid having to mend later. Reinforce stressed or worn areas, such as knees and elbows, before the fabric tears. Repair small holes or tears before they get bigger.
- Always remove stitches carefully (with a seam ripper, scissors, or pin) and mark the original stitching line with a fabric-marking pen or chalk.

How to Remove Stitches

with a seam ripper: Insert the point of the seam ripper under the stitch so the top/ball of the seam ripper is above the stitch. Gently push the seam ripper under the stitch to cut the thread.

with embroidery scissors: With small, pointed scissors, clip the stitching from the right side of the fabric. Ease one of the scissor points under the stitch and cut. Clip every third stitch and then pull the seam apart and remove the loose threads.

with a pin: For very small stitches, use a pin to pull the stitch away from the fabric and then cut it with small, pointed scissors.

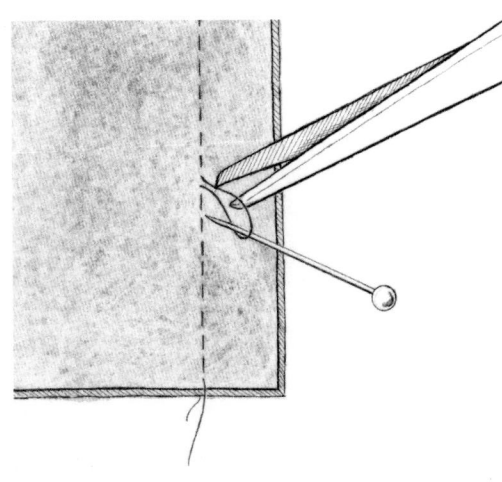

basting methods

Whether you mend by hand or by machine, you need to baste—with stitches, pins, or tape—to temporarily hold together the layers of fabric. There are several basting methods, so choose the one that works best for your project.

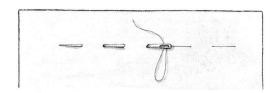

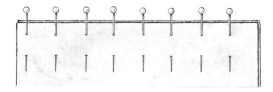

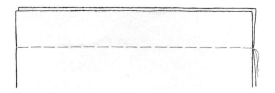

hand-basting: Baste by hand when the area you're repairing is difficult to reach, you're matching a pattern or plaid, or pins would get in the way.

Thread the needle but don't knot the end. Insert the needle in and out of the surface of the fabric to make several evenly spaced, $1/2$" (1.3 cm) long running stitches. Pull the needle through and repeat.

pin-basting: Place pins perpendicular to the stitching line, about every $1/2$" (1.3 cm), to secure a small area.

fabric glue: A glue stick or water-soluble glue, packaged in a tube applicator, temporarily holds fabric layers together to make it easier to sew the permanent stitches precisely.

machine-basting: This technique is effective for gathering and for holding long, straight seams. Adjust the machine-stitch length to the longest straight stitch—3 to 6 stitches per inch (2.5 cm).

basting tape: This very narrow tape has adhesive on both sides with removable paper backing. (Some varieties can be left in place and washed away later in the laundry.) Simply position the tape and press it in place with your fingers. Avoid stitching through it, as it will gum up the needle.

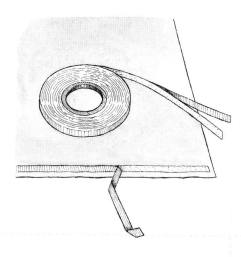

hand-sewing

Mending by hand is easy. It's the best method when repairing a small or hard-to-reach area (such as narrow sleeves or one layer of several fabric layers), or when the pattern or design of the fabric requires careful matching.

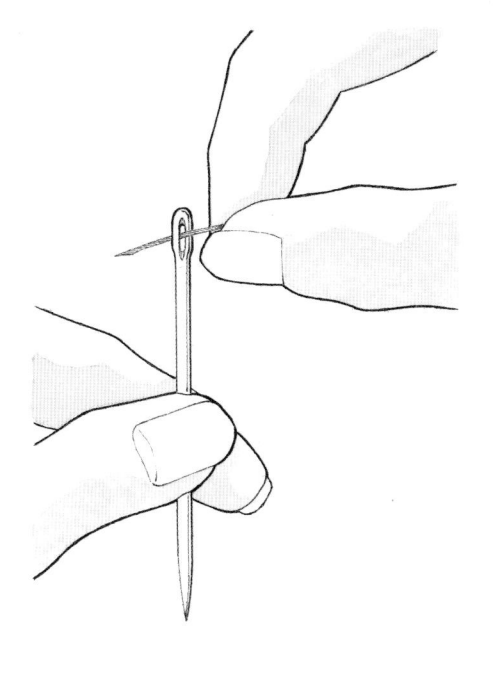

Sewing Tips

- When reattaching buttons or snaps, use a double strand of thread. For sewing seams or basting, use a single strand. Cut the thread 18" to 22" (45.5 to 56 cm) long. A longer strand will fray or tangle as you work.

- If you are sewing with a single thread, knot only one end of the thread.

- If you are sewing with a double thread (buttons, snaps), knot both ends together.

- Keep hand stitches close to together—from 12 to 15 stitches per inch (2.5 cm).

- When you can, bury or hide the thread knot between two layers of fabric, as shown below.

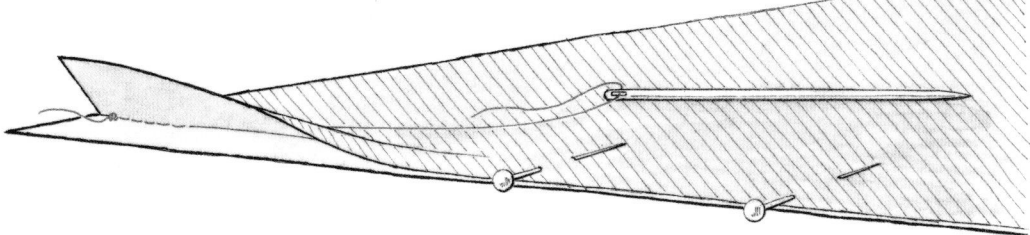

Threading a Needle

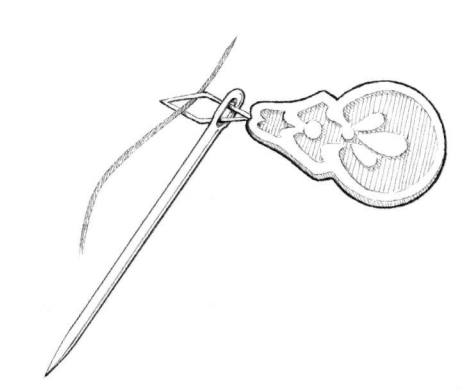

by hand: Cut the thread at an angle to make it easier to thread through the eye of the needle. Hold the thread between your thumb and forefinger, about 1/4" (6 mm) from the cut end. Push the thread through the eye of the needle. Wet or twist the thread end if you have trouble inserting it.

with a needle threader: Slide the wire loop of the needle threader through the eye of the needle. Insert the thread through the wire loop and pull the wire and thread back through the needle eye. Slide the wire threader off the thread.

To prevent the thread from pulling out of the needle as you sew, hold the needle with its eye between your thumb and middle finger. Position your forefinger in front to steer the needle's point.

securing hand stitches

When you are hand-basting you don't need to secure the end of the thread because you will be removing the stitches. For all other types of hand-sewing, secure your stitches at the beginning and end of each seam.

Securing the Beginning of a Seam

tie a thread knot: Wrap the thread loosely around your index finger one or two times and hold the loop in place with your thumb. Twist the threads and roll the loop off by sliding your finger toward the base of your thumb. Pull the loop to form a knot.

backstitch: Form two or three small backstitches (see page 18) on the wrong side of the fabric that are invisible on the right side. Leave a small loop. Take another backstitch in the same place and run the needle through the thread loop, as shown in the drawing. Pull the thread tight.

Securing the End of a Seam

backstitch: Backstitch as at the beginning of a seam, using two or three small backstitches (see page 18) on the wrong side of the fabric.

tie a thread knot: Form a thread loop at the end of the stitching on the wrong side, close to the fabric. Pull the needle through the loop, keeping the thread loop close to the fabric. Pull and tighten the knot.

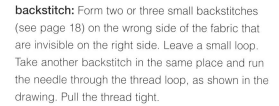

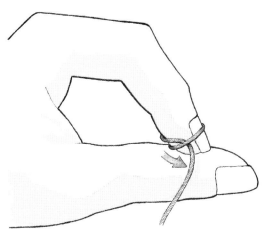

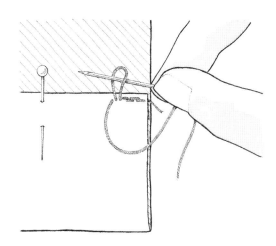

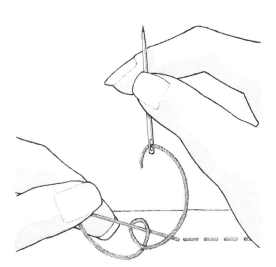

If the knot comes through the fabric, tie a second knot over the first one.

hand stitches

Hand-sewing is quick and efficient, particularly when you need to match surface patterns, when the work area is small and tight, or when you don't want visible stitches on the right side of the fabric. To stitch by hand, thread a hand needle with 18" (45.7 cm) of thread (see page 16).

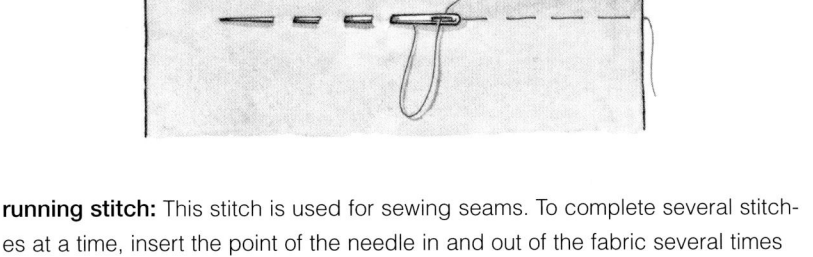

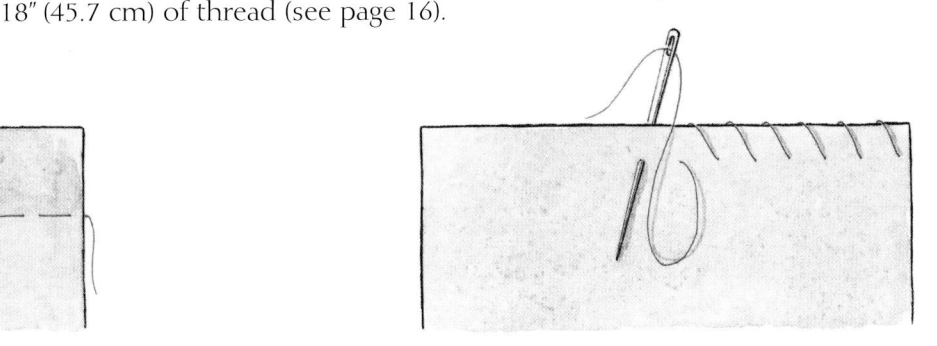

running stitch: This stitch is used for sewing seams. To complete several stitches at a time, insert the point of the needle in and out of the fabric several times before pulling the thread through. Keep the stitches and the spaces between them small and even.

overcast stitch: This stitch is well suited for mending or clean-finishing frayed or raveling edges, a repair that will strengthen the seam. Form a series of close, evenly spaced, diagonal stitches 1/4" (6 mm) deep by passing the thread over and around the fabric edge.

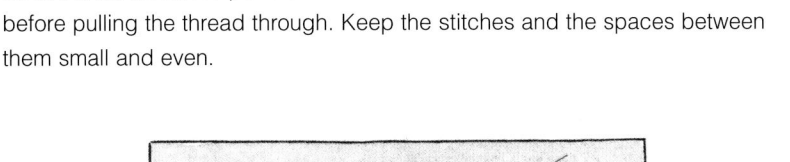

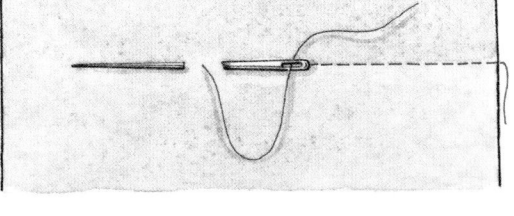

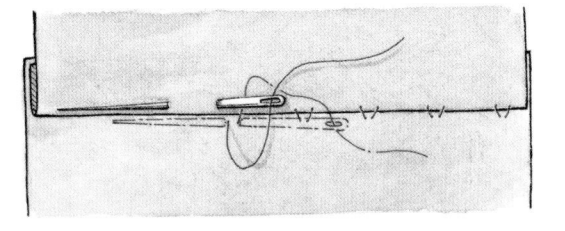

backstitch: This very strong stitch is also used for seams. Bring the needle and thread to the right side of the fabric. Insert the needle 1/16" to 1/8" (1.6 to 3 mm) behind the point where the thread exited the fabric. Then bring the needle out through the fabric that same distance in front of that point. Repeat, inserting the needle into the previous exit point for each stitch.

slip stitch: This stitch is handy for hemming and closing openings. Insert the needle inside the fabric fold and bring it out through the folded edge. Insert the needle through two or three threads of the bottom fabric. Repeat, alternating from fold to fabric with each stitch.

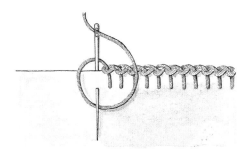

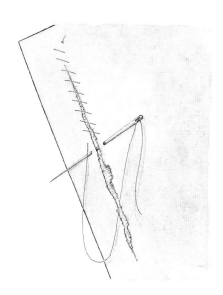

buttonhole stitch: This overedge stitch is used to make hand-sewn buttonholes or to finish other raw edges.

Insert the needle from the back to the front about 1/8" (3 mm) from the cut fabric edge. Wrap the thread under the eye of the needle and behind the point of the needle. Pull the needle through the thread so a loop forms along the fabric edge.

Repeat with closely spaced, even stitches along the cut fabric edge.

sloating stitch: This is a series of parallel stitches worked on the wrong side to repair tears in medium- to heavyweight fabrics. The stitches are invisible from the right side and look like small, slanted stitches on the wrong side.

Secure the stitch 1/2" (1.3 cm) before the tear with a small knot or two or three small backstitches. Working from top to bottom, insert the needle 1/16" (2 mm) from the torn edge and work it through the tear so it comes out 1/16" (2 mm) from the tear on the opposite side.

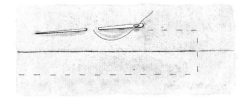

Repeat with the second stitch 1/16" (2 mm) below the first, never piercing the right side of the fabric, and only picking up a few threads on each side of the tear. Continue stitching to 1/2" (1.3 cm) beyond the end of the tear, backstitch to secure.

pick stitch: This stitch is a variation of the backstitch, perfect for inserting zippers by hand. Working from the right side of the fabric, secure the stitching with a backstitch.

Insert the needle behind the point at which the thread comes out of the fabric and bring it out 1/8" (3 mm) to 1/4" (6 mm) to the left of the same point. This stitching method leaves very small, evenly spaced stitches on the right side of the fabric.

machine-sewing

A sewing machine makes quick work of mending and repair jobs. No matter how basic your machine, it will enable you to make all sorts of neat, sturdy repairs. Familiarize yourself with your machine, and you won't dread stitching up tears, darning or patching holes, or altering items.

- Be sure your machine is threaded properly and that the stitch looks smooth and even on both sides. To check, sew a test row of stitches on a piece of scrap fabric.

- Position the repair area under the needle so the bulk of the fabric is to the left of the needle.

- Control the larger part of the fabric with your left hand, and use your right hand to guide and control the fabric under the needle.

- Sew a straight stitch with a length of 8 to 12 stitches per inch (2.5 cm).

- If the fabric is heavy, set the machine for a longer stitch length, about 6 to 10 stitches per inch (2.5 cm). If the fabric is lightweight, set the machine to 12 to 14 stitches per inch (2.5 cm).

- Avoid tangled thread at the beginning of the seam by holding both threads to the back or side of the presser foot until you take the first few stitches.

- Begin and end stitching with the needle in the highest position.

- Leave the needle in the fabric and lift the presser foot to turn a corner.

- Backstitch 2 or 3 stitches at the beginning and the end of the seam to secure or lock the stitching.

- Raise the presser foot and pull the fabric out at the end of the seam. If the bobbin thread doesn't release easily, turn the handwheel counterclockwise slightly.

- Clip thread ends at the beginning and end of the seam, close to the fabric.

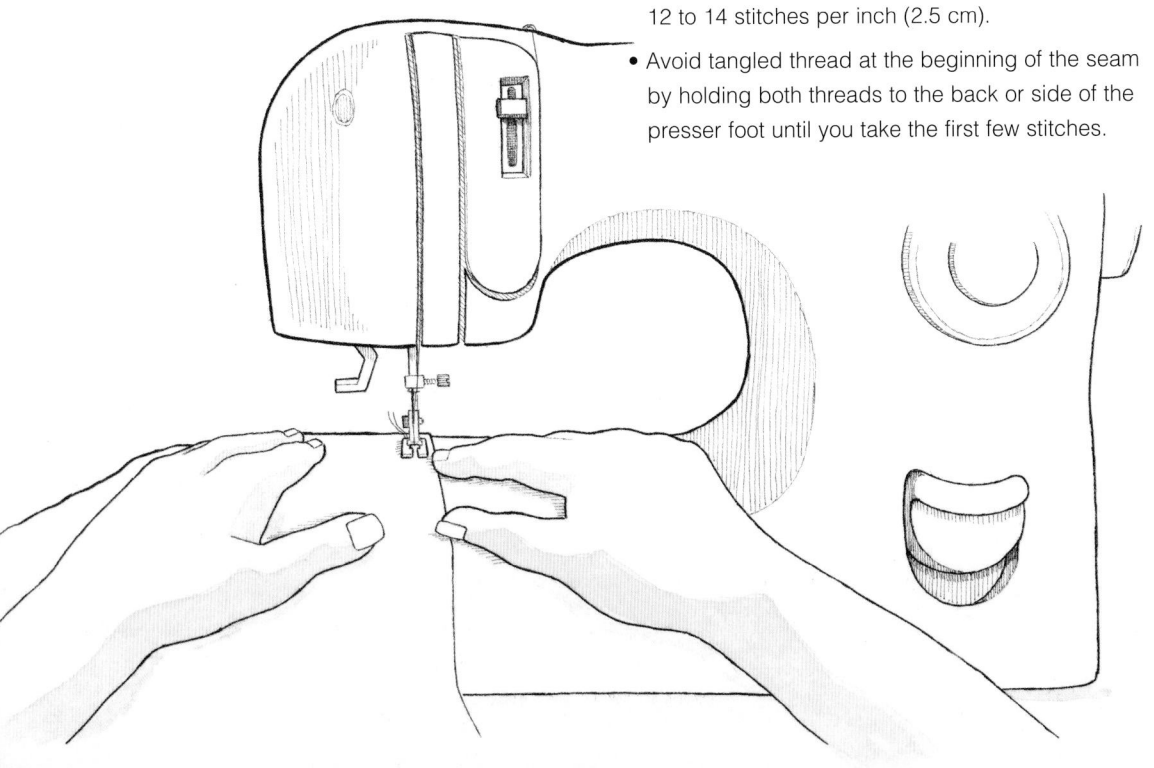

machine stitches

You can do almost all your mending with a straight or zigzag stitch. If the fabric is a knit or stretch woven, use a zigzag or stretch stitch. Match the color of the thread and the length of the stitches with the stitching that is already on the item you are mending. Test on scrap fabric first.

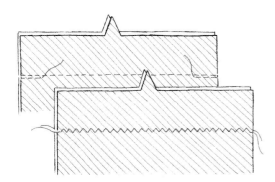

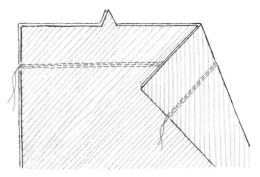

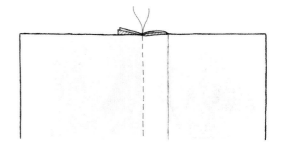

straight stitch: This basic stitch is perfect for most sewing. Choose the longest stitch for basting (see page 15) and a shorter stitch (8 to 12 stitches per inch [2.5 cm]) for regular sewing. Set the length of the stitch so that it matches the rest of the stitching. Be sure to backstitch to secure the beginning and end of the stitching.

zigzag stitch: This stitch is great for seaming stretch fabrics. It helps prevent puckers and broken stitches by building stretch into the seam. Choose a stitch length that is compatible with the weight of the fabric (longer stitches for heavy fabrics, shorter stitches for lightweight fabrics). The zigzag stitch is also commonly worked along the raw edges of fabric to clean-finish them.

straight stretch stitch: This specialty stitch is built into some sewing machines. Test the stitch on scrap fabric first, because it is difficult to rip out. It can have the appearance of three, very closely spaced, parallel rows of straight stitches (as shown in the drawing), or two forward stitches and one backward stitch.

To make bar tacks for reinforcing corners or openings, use a wide, short zigzag.

topstitch: To topstitch, sew straight stitches on the right side of the fabric to emphasize a detail, to hold seam allowances in place, or to create design interest.

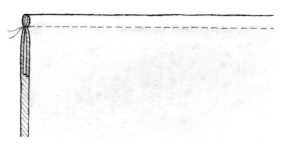

edge stitch: Edge stitching is topstitching that is close to the finished edge or seam line (1/16" to 1/8" [2 to 3 mm]). You can use a blind-stitch foot to ensure even stitching.

fixing with fusibles

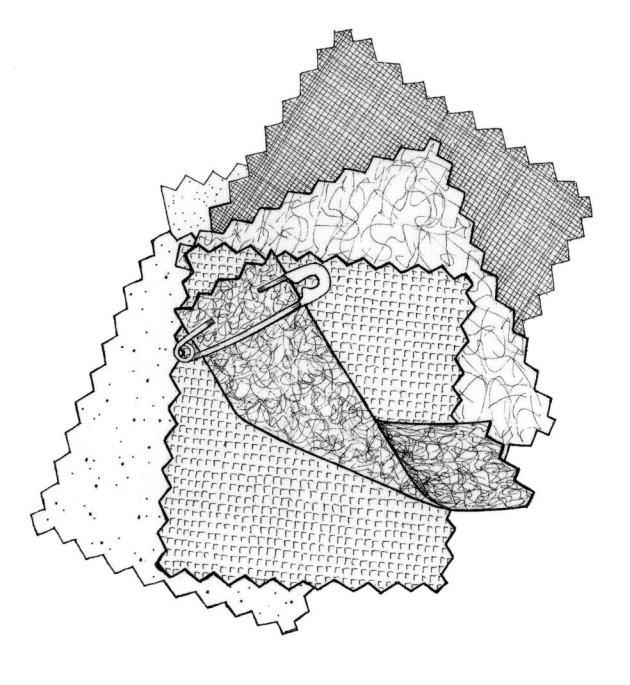

Fusible products offer "no-sew" mending and repair options. Fusibles can help you mend, add stability, attach trim, and support fabrics that are worn thin. Here are a few to keep handy for five-minute fix-ups.

fusible interfacing: Choose this adhesive-backed fabric to add shape and crispness to limp fabric, stability to stretchy fabric, and durability to worn fabrics. Woven, knit, and nonwoven varieties offer many degrees of support and stretch.

Work with iron-on interfacing to hold tears and seams together to make them easier to sew. You can also apply it as an interior patch on fabric that needs support.

fusible web: Sold by the yard or in precut strips, with or without paper backing, this heat-activated product is used to fuse two layers together.

Paper–backed fusible web is fused in two steps. Position it on the first layer and press. Remove the paper backing and fuse the second layer over the first.

Fusible web without paper backing is placed between two pieces of fabric, or between fabric and trim, and fused in one step.

fusible mending tape: Mending tape is heavier than fusible web and works to close a tear. After fusing it in place, stitch over it to reinforce. Fusible mending tape comes in precut strips and patches.

fusible stabilizer: Stabilizer is used to temporarily stiffen a fabric area so that you can stitch on it. After stitching you can tear it away or, in the case of wash-away products, dissolve the stabilizer with a damp cloth. Stabilizer is helpful when you are darning a hole or tear and when you are embroidering by hand or machine.

fusible trim, fusible drapery tapes, fusible rhinestones, and fusible Velcro: These products are designed for convenience. They are like their sew-on cousins, but they have fusible adhesive on the back. Just position them and fuse, following the manufacturer's instructions. Apply them to cover stains or holes or to restyle existing draperies and other home décor.

Fusing Tips

- Follow the manufacturer's instructions and recommendations for heat, pressure, moisture, and drying time.

- Prewash the fabric to remove sizing.

- Prewash the interfacing to eliminate the possibility of shrinkage. Soak it in a basin with hot (not boiling) water for about thirty minutes. Squeeze out excess moisture and hang it to dry.

- Test a small piece of the fusible on the seam or hem allowance or on another inconspicuous area. Make sure the fusible doesn't change the feel of the fabric and that the fused layers don't tear apart.

- Protect the fabric and the sole plate of the iron by placing a press cloth, brown paper, or pressing paper on top of the fabric.

- Place the interfacing (or any fusible with adhesive on one side), adhesive side down, on the wrong side of the fabric. Cover it with a damp press cloth.

  With your iron set to the temperature suggested for the type of fabric you are working with, press (don't move the iron) one section for about fifteen seconds. Lift and repeat until the whole piece is fused in place.

- To maximize the efficiency of the fusible, press on both sides after the initial fusing process.

- You can use fusibles to prevent or minimize raveling and further tearing.

- Fusibles add stiffness and weight, so they are not always suitable for sheer and lightweight fabrics. There are special interfacings specifically made for sheer fabrics.

- Fuse large pieces, like a table runner or a window shade, by covering your kitchen table with a thin blanket and an old sheet to create a large pressing surface.

- Fusibles have different bonding strength. Make sure the weight and strength of the fusible matches the weight of the fabric.

- Avoid using fusible web that is too heavy. The adhesive might seep through the fabric and leave residue on the right side.

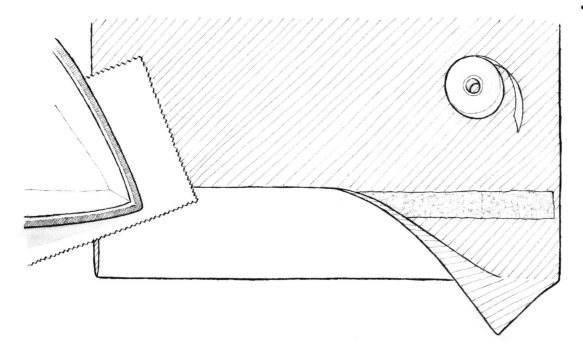

Mark a press cloth with "This side up for fusing" and always use it when working with iron-on adhesive products. You'll avoid getting glue on your iron.

about darning

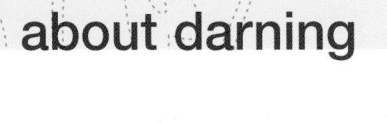

Darning is the weaving of thread or yarn across a hole in a piece of fabric to fill and conceal the hole. You can also darn across a thin or worn area of fabric to strengthen it, to prevent a hole from forming, and to close a fabric tear.

For support as you darn, place the damaged fabric over a darning egg or mushroom—or other firm, rounded object, such as a smooth rock, light bulb, piece of cardboard, or plastic ball. Stretch the fabric slightly as you stitch.

• Work with darning needles (see page 10), which are longer than other hand-sewing needles and extend across the diameter of a hole more easily.

For fine fabrics and small holes, work with a smaller darning needle. For knits, wools, and heavier fabrics, choose a longer darning needle with a bigger eye.

• Try to find thread or yarn that matches the color, weight, and texture of the fabric. For lightweight woven fabrics, look for silk, cotton, or polyester/cotton thread.

Embroidery floss is a good alternative to thread because you can separate the plies to make the darning strand as thick or thin as you want. Wool or crewel yarn is suitable for wool coats, socks, and blankets.

• Pull threads from a cut edge inside the item, such as the seam allowances or hem, if you can't purchase matching thread or yarn.

• Darn solid-color fabric with matching thread or yarn so that the repair is barely visible. A multi-color pattern is a little harder to darn invisibly. You can try to shade the darned area by using two or three different colored threads. For the least obtrusive repair, you may need to simply patch the garment (see page 30).

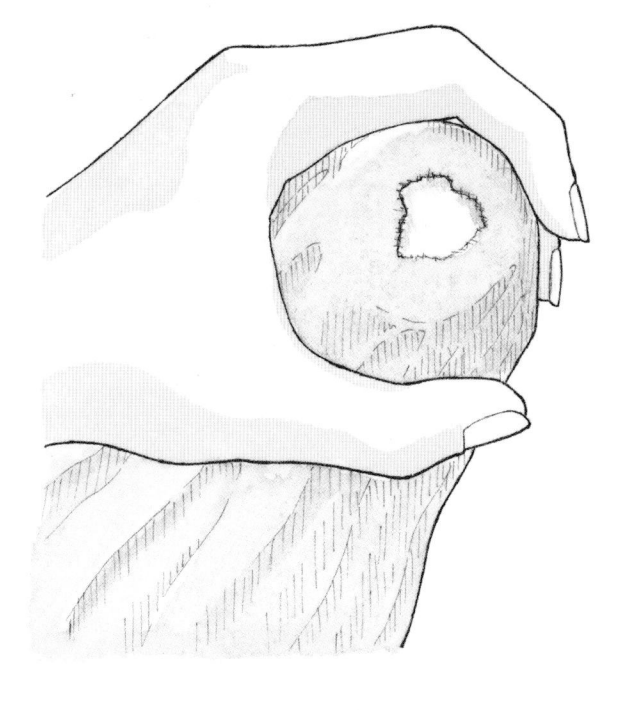

- If a hole is small and unobtrusive, seal it by dabbing it with a liquid fray preventer, such as Fray Check.

- If the hole is large, place a small piece of net or fine muslin in a matching color under the hole on the wrong side and catch it in all the darning stitches. The small piece of fabric provides support for the darning stitches.

- When you work darning stitches, do not pull them tight or you will close the hole and distort the fabric. Keep stitches taut—but not tight—so they span the hole.

- Make sure the darning stitches cover the hole and the surrounding, usually weakened, fabric, too.

- Shape the outer edges of the darned area slightly, so the stitches don't stress the same fabric threads on every stitch. Avoid darning in a perfect square.

- Space the stitches as close together as possible to form a tight weave.

- Before darning a burn hole in fabric, trim away the burned or frayed area first, as shown in drawing below.

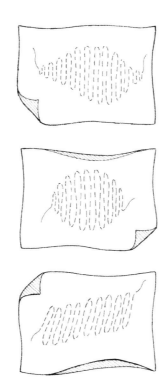

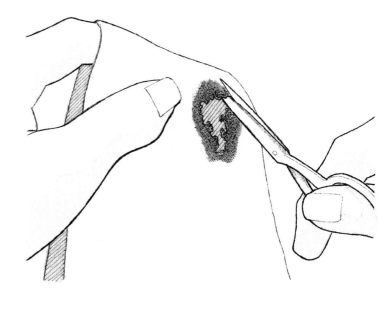

For a casual, "distressed" look, try darning jeans with contrasting color thread.

darning by hand

The best way to hand-darn a hole or tear is by inserting a patch of fabric or fusible interfacing inside the item and darning over the patch. A small hole or tear doesn't require a patch.

Darning a Hole by Hand

1 Thread a needle. Support the weakened fabric near the hole by sewing a line of short running stitches around the perimeter of the hole, about 1/4" (6 mm) from the edge.

2 Place the hole over a hard surface, such as a darning egg or a smooth rock, to stretch it and support it. Sew closely spaced, long, straight stitches across the hole, starting and ending each stitch at the stitches that encircle the hole.

3 With a new thread, weave the threaded needle in and out of, and at right angles to, the first layer of stitches, picking up some garment threads as you go. To finish, pull the thread to the wrong side and run it under previous stitches. Clip the thread.

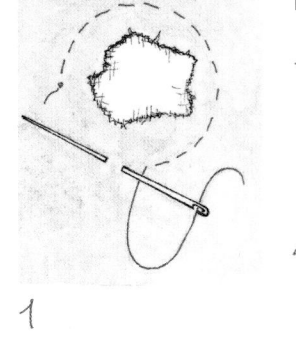

1

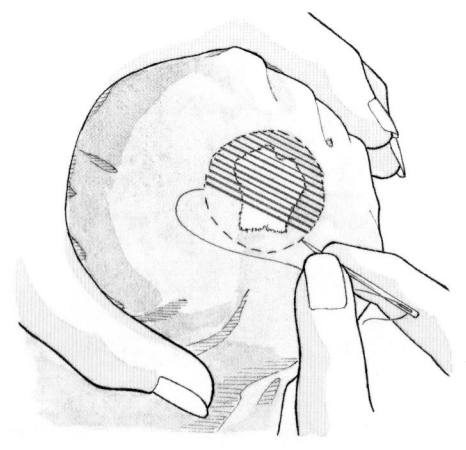

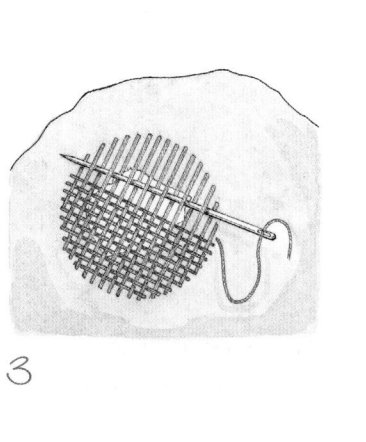

2

3

Darning a Tear by Hand

1 Trim away loose threads. Working on the wrong side, bring the fabric edges together. Sew the sloating stitch (see page 19) to close the tear, beginning and ending 1/2" (1.3 cm) beyond the tear. Backstitch or knot at the end of the tear.

2 If the tear is in a high-stress location, reinforce it by turning the tear upside down and sewing a second row of sloating stitches to form crisscrosses over the first row.

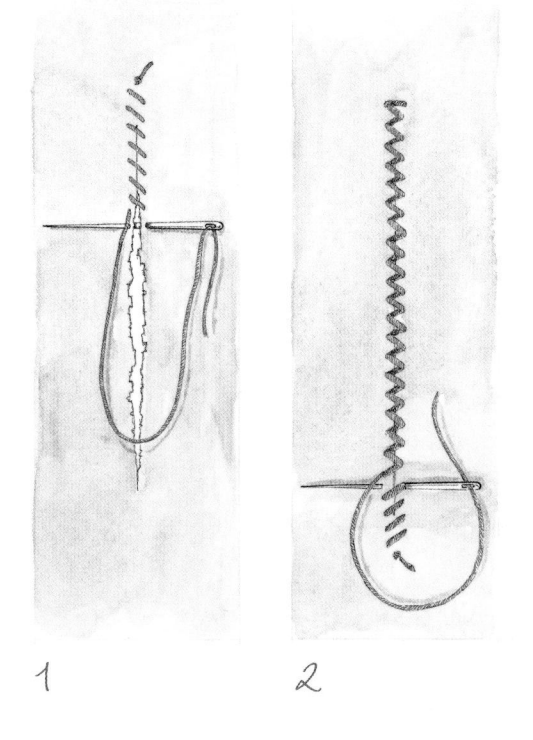

1   2

darning knit fabrics

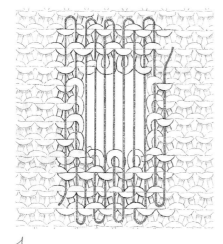

1

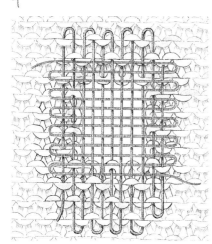

2

Darning knits is much the same as darning woven fabrics. You'll get a much better result if you do it by hand rather than by machine. Sweater-type knits are surprisingly forgiving of darning—their lofty texture conceals darning stitches nicely. Whether your sweater has a hole, a moth hole, or a burn, you can salvage it with a minimum of effort. The key to successful darning is to work with yarns that match the garment in weight, texture, and color.

1. Tuck all loose yarn ends to the wrong side of the garment. Don't clip them, or you'll risk a bigger hole. Starting above and to the side of the tear, weave stitches through the existing stitches and then across the hole. Continue stitching across the entire hole and 1/2" (1.3 cm) beyond it. Don't pull the stitches tight.

2. To finish the repair, weave stitches through the first stitches and perpendicular to them, across the hole and 1/2" (1.3 cm) beyond the edges of the hole. Weave broken yarns into the darning stitches on the wrong side.

darning by machine

Darning by machine requires a few machine adjustments, which enable you to control the movement of the fabric under the needle. Remove the standard presser foot and lower or cover the feed dogs, following the instructions for your machine.

Preparing the Fabric

Mount the damaged fabric in an embroidery hoop: Sandwich the fabric between the hoop's two rings to hold it taut. The hoop will allow you to slide the fabric back and forth under the needle to form the stitches. Darning by machine takes some practice, so practice on scrap fabric first. Machine darning stitches are usually visible from the right side.

Preparing the machine

1   Loosen the upper thread tension slightly (follow the instructions in your owner's manual).

2   Sew without a presser foot or replace the presser foot with a darning foot (see page 13).

3   Lower the feed dogs or attach a darning plate to cover the feed dogs (refer to your owner's manual).

4   Set the machine for a medium-length straight stitch.

Darning a Hole

Center the hole in an embroidery hoop, with the right side up. If the hole is larger than 5/8" (1.5 cm), baste a fabric patch or a piece of stabilizer over the hole on the wrong side of the fabric.

Hand-sew short running stitches around the perimeter of the hole, as shown in the drawing below.

Slip the embroidery hoop under the needle and work rows of straight stitches back and forth over the hole by moving the fabric under the needle. The stitches should be very close together.

Turn the hoop 90 degrees and repeat the sewing to cover the first layer of stitches. Trim away excess fabric or remove the stabilizer after the stitching is complete.

Darning a Small Tear

For tears less than 1" (2.5 cm) long, pin or hold the edges of the tear together and stitch a single row of wide, zigzag stitches directly over the tear.

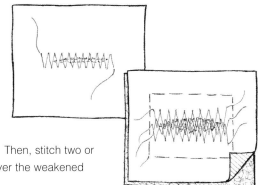

Darning a Large Tear

Pin, hand-baste, or fuse stabilizer behind the tear. From the right side, zigzag directly over the tear. Then, stitch two or three parallel rows on each side of the first row to cover the weakened area.

Fusing a Tear

If you don't want to see darning stitches in the item or garment, fuse interfacing to the wrong side of the fabric, following the manufacturer's application instructions. Position a press cloth on top of the interfacing to protect the iron.

In some cases the interfacing will hold the tear closed, but not always. A large tear or a tear located in an area that's subject to stress will also need darning by machine or hand over the interfacing. Hand-wash the mended garment to eliminate the wear and tear of machine-washing.

If you don't have an embroidery hoop, place an extra layer or two of stabilizer on the wrong side of the fabric to support the stitching. Trim away excess stabilizer after darning the hole.

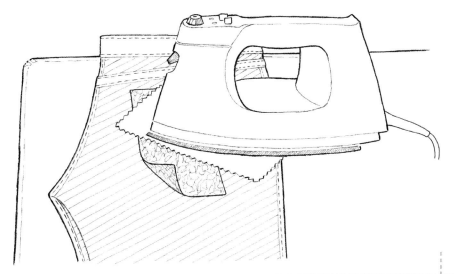

about patches

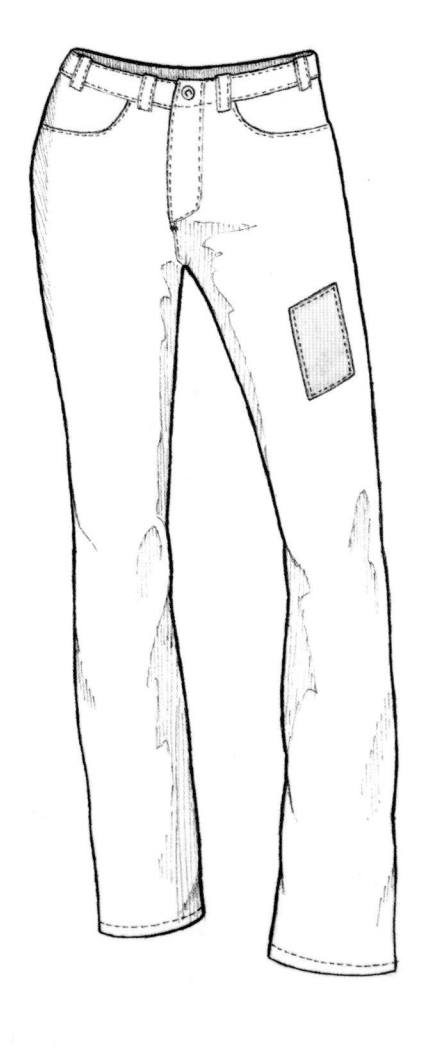

A patch is a small piece of fabric that covers, replaces, conceals, reinforces, or repairs a torn, worn, or stained area. Select fabric for a patch that's similar in weight and care requirements to the item's fabric. The patch can be sewn or fused in place on the right or wrong side of the fabric.

Decorative Effects

Make your patch a statement by using fabric in a color or pattern that contrasts with the garment fabric. Apply it on the right side of the garment. Use contrast thread for more emphasis.

Unobtrusive Repairs

Choose a matching fabric and apply the patch to the wrong side of the garment. Consider cutting fabric from the garment hem, a facing, the bottom of sleeves, or an interior pocket. Replace whatever you cut from the garment with muslin.

Tips for Patching

- Reinforce high-stress areas, like knees and elbows, with an interior patch before the garment fabric tears or wears through.

- Patch holes and tears as soon as you notice them, before they get larger.

- Consider a decorative patch or appliqué for holes that are large or in a very noticeable location (see page 87).

- Stabilize small holes on the wrong side of the fabric and cover them with beautiful buttons. Choose one button or several to create a "design detail."

- Patch pant legs and sleeves by hand if it's hard to reach the repair site by machine. Or, open the seams of the pant leg or sleeve to access the patch by machine.

fusing an iron-on patch

A store-bought fusible patch is a quick way to mend, especially worn-out knees! Refer to the fusing instructions on the packaging.

- Consider buying iron-on, ready-made patches, especially for denim fabric. You may need to edge-stitch or zigzag them as well as fuse them for long-term durability.
- Before fusing patches in place, trim square corners to round them. The rounded edges help prevent the patch from pulling away from the surface of the garment fabric.
- Work with fusible products to make iron-on patches from your own fabric (see page 22).
- If the hole or tear is large, you might need an inside patch as well, so the fusible product has something to adhere to.

To fuse a store-bought patch, cut it at least 1" (2.5 cm) larger all around than the hole or worn area. Round the corners. Trim away the frayed edges of the damaged area. Position the patch over the hole, with the fusible side down. Insert a piece of paper between the patch and the bottom layer of the garment so the patch doesn't fuse the garment closed.

Adjust the setting of the iron as recommended. Press the patch firmly by lifting and lowering the iron rather than sliding it. When the patch is cool, check that it's securely fused. If not, press it again.

For added strength, zigzag-stitch around the perimeter of the fused patch on the right side of the patch and garment.

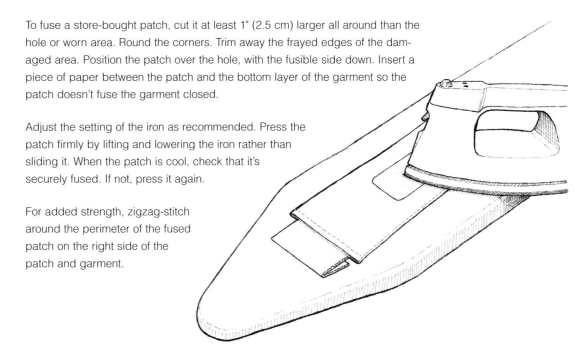

patching on the right side

Patched repairs are certainly more noticeable than darned repairs, but they are also stronger. If you don't mind that the patch is visible—or want to add a decorative touch—just sew it on the right side of jeans, work clothes, children's clothes, sport bags, tents, and workout or sports gear.

Prepare the Patch

1 Cut a patch of fabric 1" (2.5 cm) larger all around than the hole. It can be any shape.

2 If the fabric is light- to medium-weight, press under all the edges 1/2" (1.3 cm).

3 Press the area around the hole or tear and then trim away any loose threads.

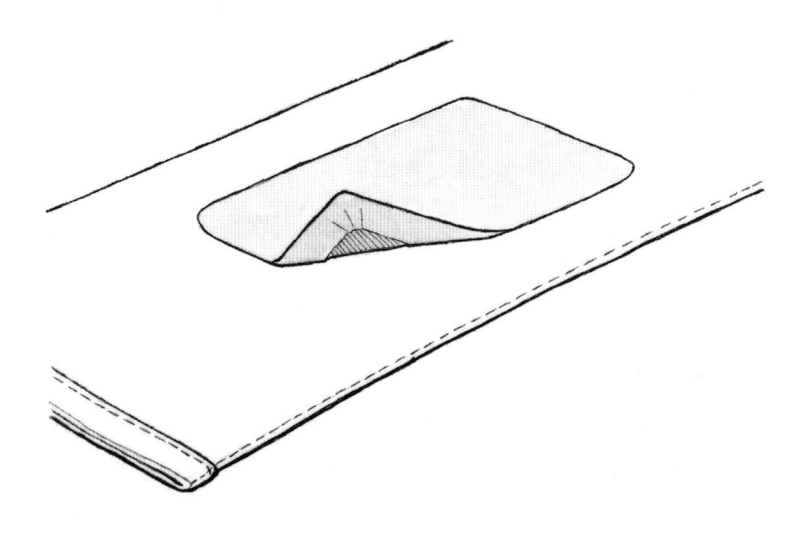

How to Machine-Sew the Patch

1 Center and pin the patch, right side up, on the right side of the garment.

2 Position the garment and patch right side up under the presser foot, with the edge of the patch slightly to the right of the needle.

3 Edge-stitch the patch to the garment (see page 21). Pivot at the corners, if there are any.

How to Hand-Sew the Patch

1 On the right side of the garment, center and pin the patch over the hole.

2 Backstitch (see page 18) the patch to the garment.

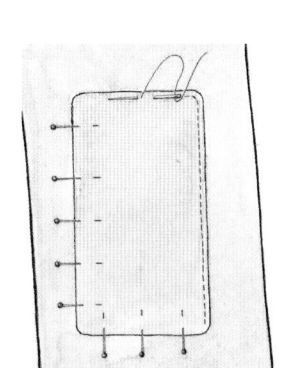

finishing the edges

If you didn't press under the edges of the patch before applying it, you'll want to finish them in one of the following ways to keep them neat through wearing, washing, and drying.

medium- to heavyweight fabric patches: Minimize bulk by attaching the patch without turning under the edges. After edge-stitching the patch to the right side of the garment, set the machine to the widest possible zigzag stitch and a stitch length between 10 and 12 stitches per inch (2.5 cm).

Attach an embroidery presser foot to the sewing machine. With the right side up, position the patch so the cut edge is slightly to the right of the needle. Sew around the patch so that the zigzag stitch spans the cut raw edge of the patch. Pivot at corners, if there are any.

patches of any weight: Edge-stitch the patch in place, leaving the edges raw. Then, outline the raw edges of the patch with decorative fabric paint.

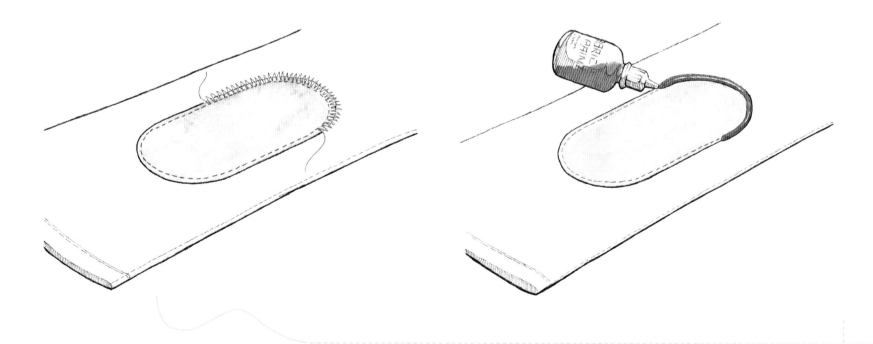

patching on the wrong side

A patch applied to the wrong side is less visible than one applied to the right side. Apply it with a fusible product or sew it. If the fabric ravels a lot, it's best to sew it (see page 35). If you are fusing the patch, you may need to reinforce the edge of the hole with small zigzag stitches or liquid fray preventer to prevent raveling. In either case, use the gentle cycle whenever you launder the mended item.

Fusing a Patch to the Wrong Side

1   Trim the ragged edges from the hole. Cut a piece of matching fabric and a piece of paper-backed fusible web, both 1/2" (1.3 cm) larger than the hole.

2   Center the fabric hole over the paper side of the fusible web. With a pencil, mark the outline of the hole through the fabric onto the paper. Cut out the outlined shape at the center of the fusible web patch to create a ring.

3   Press the fusible web ring to the right side of the fabric patch, following the manufacturer's instructions.

4   Remove the paper backing and position the patch on the wrong side of the garment, so that the right side of the fabric, but not the fusible web ring, is visible through the hole. Fuse the patch in place.

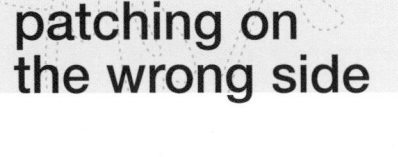

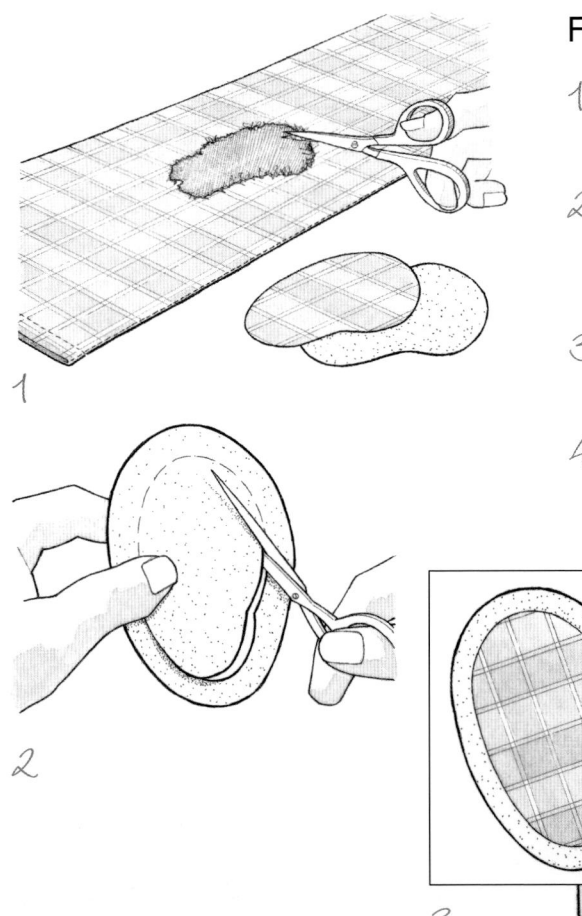

1

2

3

4

Sewing a patch to the wrong side

1   Trim the ragged edges from the hole to form a square or rectangle. Snip
½" (1.3 cm) diagonally into each corner of the hole. Cut a patch of fabric
(matching any stripes, plaids, or pattern) so that it is at least 1" (2.5 cm)
longer and wider than the hole.

2   Press the edges of the hole to the wrong side.

3   Cover the hole by pinning the patch inside the garment, right side of patch
to wrong side of garment, matching any patterns.

4   Working from the inside of the garment, machine-stitch one side of the
patch to the folded-back edge of the hole, sewing along the pressed-in
fold. Don't catch the outer layers of the garment in the stitching. Backstitch
at the beginning and end of the seam.

5   Repeat step 5 for each side. Trim the patch edges to align with the folded-
back edges of the hole. If the fabric ravels, pink or overcast the raw edges
of the seams.

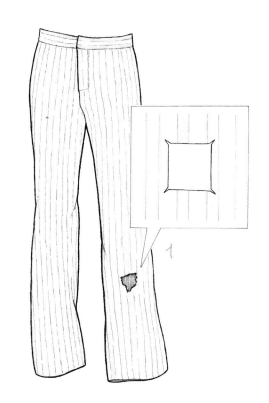

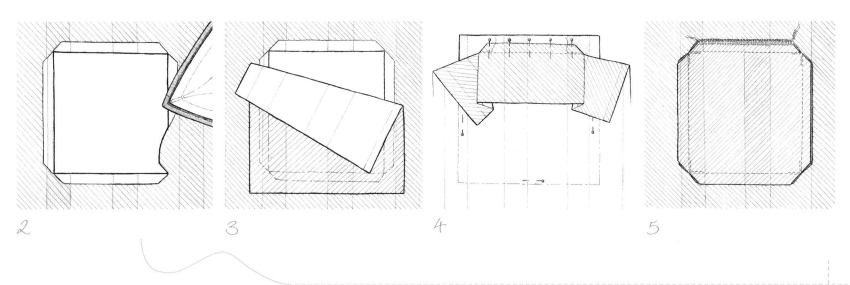

thread snags and pulls

Sometimes a snagged thread is as unsightly as a hole or tear. Both knit and woven fabrics, especially those with a loose weave structure, can get caught on jewelry, buttons, or hooks, or any number of other objects you brush against. Don't cut the pulled thread away, or you might end up with a big hole! Instead, try these methods for pushing the snagged thread back into the fabric—or at least to the wrong side where it won't show and can't get snagged again.

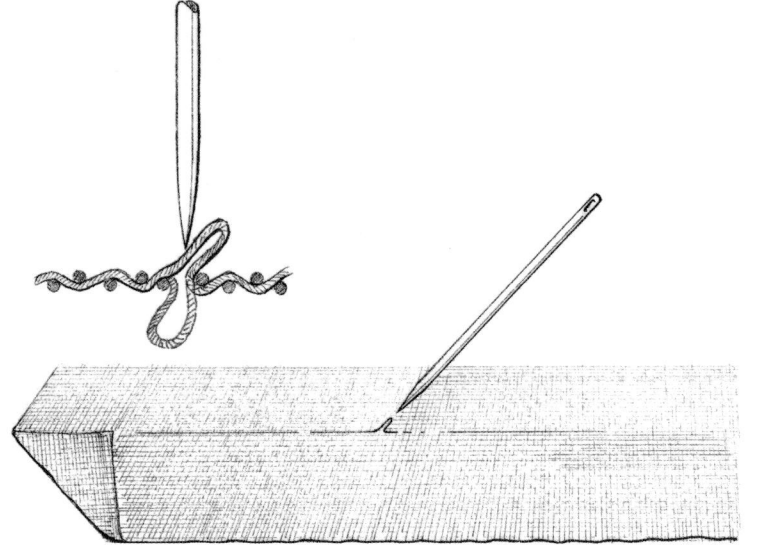

on woven fabrics: Push the thread loop to the wrong side of the garment. Manipulating the thread can be tricky on lightweight and fine fabrics, but if you work under good light it shouldn't be a problem.

Use a needle or very small crochet hook to push the snag through the other threads to the wrong side of the fabric. Hand-sew two or three backstitches over the pulled thread, or dab a liquid fray preventer on the area.

on knit fabrics: Try stretching the fabric gently, just enough so that the snag is pulled back into the fabric.

If this doesn't work, insert a small crochet hook from the wrong side of the fabric next to the snag on the right side. Catch the loop of pulled yarn in the hook and pull it to the wrong side of the fabric. Make a loop with the yarn and pull the end through to form a knot.

repairing straight seams

It's easy to repair seams—because most often they are straight lines of stitching that just need to be reinforced. You can repair seams by hand with a backstitch or machine-stitch them with a straight stitch.

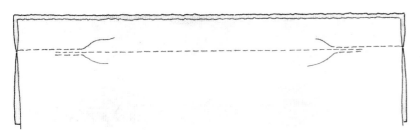
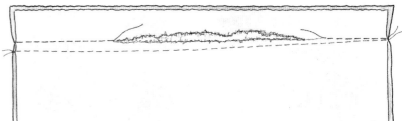

Simple Ripped Seam

Press the seam allowances together. Then cut away the broken threads. Hand- or machine-stitch across the unstitched area, following the original seam line.

Stitch 1" (2.5 cm) beyond the tear at both ends backstitching to secure the thread.

Ripped Seam with Frayed or Torn Fabric

Stabilize the fabric on both sides of the seam before you attempt to fix it. Cut two pieces of medium-weight fusible interfacing that are long enough to cover the tear and about 1" (2.5 cm) wide.

Fuse one piece to the wrong side of the fabric on each side of the seam, pulling together the torn edges of the tear to bond them closed with the fusible. Restitch the seam as you would for a simple ripped seam.

Ripped Seam in a Loose-Fitting Item

If there is enough extra room in the item or garment, sew a slightly wider seam allowance.

Begin the new line of stitching well above the end of the tear and parallel to the original line of stitching, increasing the amount of fabric in the seam allowance. The tear in the fabric will be concealed and enough out of the way so it won't cause further damage.

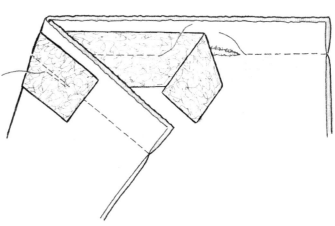

reinforcing stressed seams

When a seam rips in a high-stress location—such as an underarm, pocket, dart, or vent—it is important to reinforce the fabric, so the seam doesn't rip again.

Darts

To repair a dart, turn the garment inside out and pin along the fold of the dart. Redraw the stitching line with a fabric-marking pen. Straight-stitch by machine or backstitch by hand along the marked line, tapering gently toward the point. Tie the thread ends into a knot at the point.

Vents and Slits

If only the vent seam is ripped, turn the garment inside out and stitch over the previous seam line, as you would for a simple straight seam (see page 37).

Unfortunately, when a vent or slit rips open, the fabric frequently rips, too. Reinforce the fabric with a patch before repairing the seam. Remove the stitches that hold the vent facings in place, and press the facings and seam allowances together.

Patch the torn fabric by applying fusible interfacing on the wrong side. Resew the seam. Press the vent facings back into position, then hand-sew them to secure.

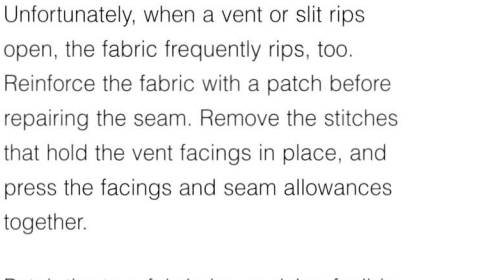

Underarm Seams

Underarms often rip because they are so well used. Resew the seam patch, then patch.

Cut a lightweight muslin patch in the shape of a diamond, about 4" (10.2 cm) long and 1 1/2" (4 cm) at its widest point. Press 1/4" (6 mm) of the edges to the wrong side of the fabric. Center and pin the patch on top of the underarm seam. Stitch along the patch edges and over the seam line, through all layers.

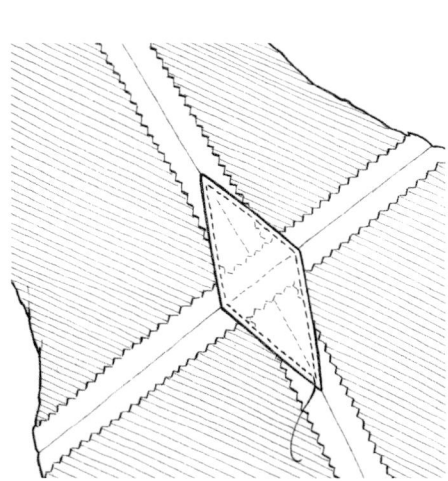

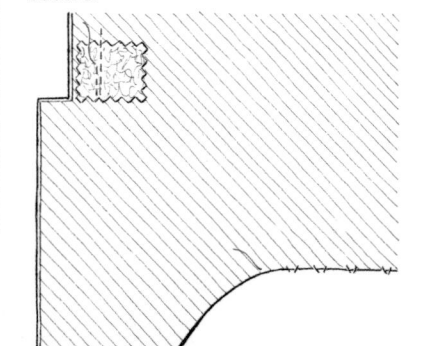

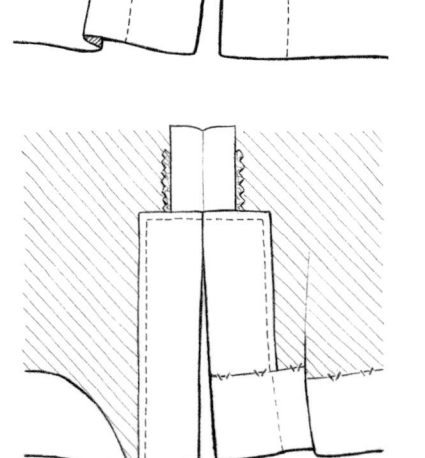

mending
patch pockets

The edge stitching that holds a pocket in place sometimes breaks—most often, at the top corners—because of the stress the wearer causes by inserting hands, keys, and other heavy or bulky objects. You can reattach a patch pocket with a hand-worked backstitching, but a machine-stitched repair will be stronger.

When the stitching on a patch pocket breaks, remove all the strands of broken thread. Pin the pocket to the fabric and restitch on the previous stitching line, starting and finishing 1" (2.5 cm) beyond the intact stitches. Backstitch at the beginning and end of your stitching line.

When the top corner of a patch pocket comes unstitched, you need to add a reinforcing fabric patch on the inside of the garment. Cut a small square of muslin and fusible web. Fuse the fabric patch to the wrong side of the garment, over the weakened or torn area.

Then, restitch the top corners with one of several reinforcing stitch options. You can either:

- Stitch a narrow zigzag stitch for about $5/8$" (1.5 cm), just inside the edge stitching.

- Sew a small triangle of straight stitches. To make sure they are all the same size, measure and mark $3/4$" (2 cm) from the corner across the top and side edges. Join the markings with a diagonal stitching line.

- Backstitch $5/8$" (1.5 cm) directly over the edge- or topstitching.

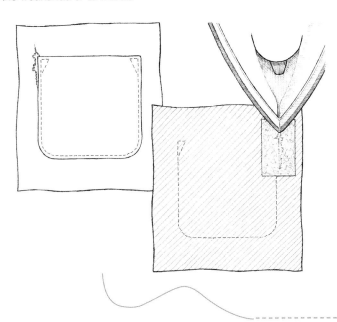

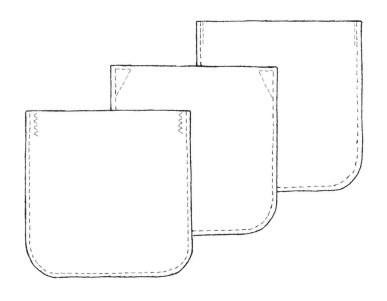

repairing in-seam pockets

In-seam pockets can tear either in the bag of the pocket or at the garment seam. Both types of tears are easy to fix.

in-seam pocket bags: Pocket bags are subject to a lot of wear and tear. If you fix the broken stitching as soon as it rips, you won't lose anything out of your pocket.

Machine- or hand-stitch directly over the torn stitching line, beginning and ending 1" (2.5 cm) beyond the rip. Be sure to backstitch at the beginning and end of the new stitching.

in-seam pockets at the garment seam: The bottom of the pocket opening is subject to a lot of friction. If the garment seam starts to open, turn the garment inside out and press the side seam allowances together, with the pocket extending away from the seam.

Re-stitch over the seam line, starting and ending 1" (2.5 cm) beyond the torn area, and backstitching at both ends. If the fabric has ripped, fuse a patch over the broken stitching to strengthen the area, then restitch the seam. Backstitch at the beginning and end of the new stitching.

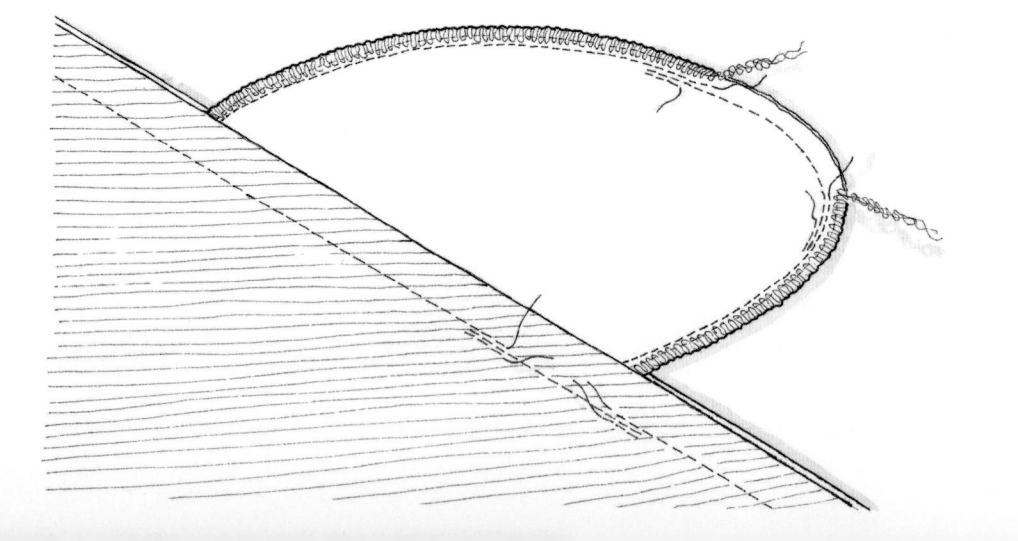

If a pocket bag is badly tattered, cut it away and sew the pocket closed.

reattaching decorative trim

Decorative trim is designed to be seen, so when it frays, tears, or comes undone, it's usually pretty noticeable—and unattractive. Fix the trim right away with a few stitches or fabric glue, and it will be as good as new. Notice how the trim was originally attached and follow the same method for the repair.

frayed ends: Ribbon, cording, and other flat trims tend to fray if the ends are not caught in a seam. Zigzag-stitch over the ends with matching thread, to prevent more raveling and to keep the ends flat and less noticeable. You can also dab liquid fray preventer, fabric glue, or even clear nail polish on the ends.

loose trim: Secure a loose section of trim or appliqué with basting tape, fabric glue, or a fusible web (see page 22). If the trim was sewn in place, stitch back over the missing stitches. If it was glued in place, apply pressure and heat, if necessary, to make sure the adhesive sets.

lost trim: Rhinestones, sequins, and beads often fall off the fabric surface. It's fairly easy to find matches in fabric and craft stores. Sew or glue the replacements in place (see pages 88 and 89).

If you can't find acceptable replacement pieces, you might want to consider replacing all of the rhinestones, sequins, or beads so they match—a big job! You can also remove a piece from a less obvious area of the item and reposition it where you need it.

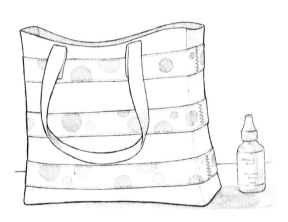

repairing edge finishes

Edge finishes and embellishments are often subject to a lot of wear—even when the rest of the item is still in good shape. Repairing the edges of a garment, accessory, or soft furnishing will extend their life.

piping or welting comes unstitched: Piping or welting is inserted into a seam. Sometimes the seam opens, letting the trim hang loose. To put the item back together, turn it inside out. Pin the seam closed, along the previous stitching, sandwiching the piping in place as it originally was.

Attach a zipper foot to your machine. Begin and end stitching 1/2" (1.3 cm) beyond the tear, and stitch the seam closed.

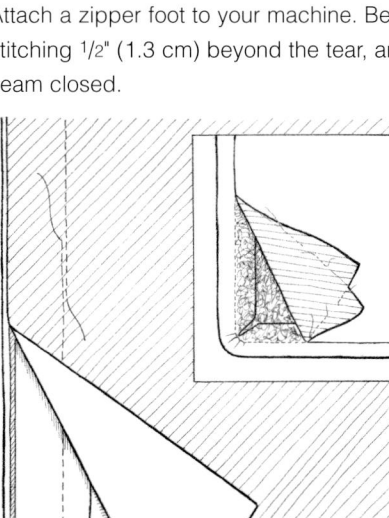

binding tears away from the fabric edge: Sometimes the fabric edge pulls out of its binding; this is common with the satin binding on blankets. With a seam ripper, remove the stitches that hold the binding in place 2" (5 cm) beyond the rip in both directions.

If the fabric edge is frayed, fuse a narrow strip of fusible interfacing to it to create a more stable edge. Trim the interfacing so it fits in the binding.

Fold the binding over the edge and pin. Edge-stitch the binding, starting and ending 1" (2.5 cm) beyond the opening.

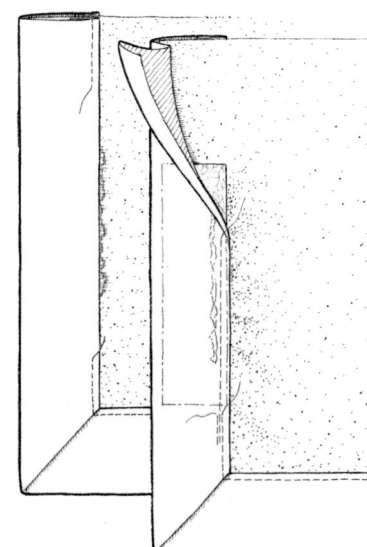
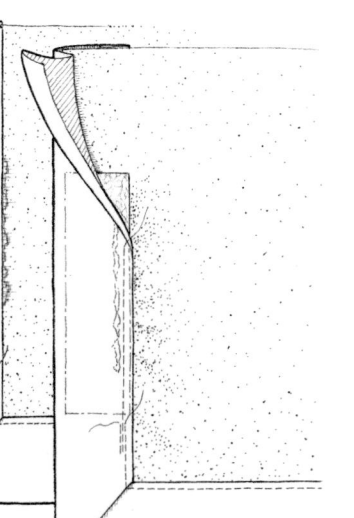

damaged trim: A snag, rip, or hole in a decorative trim is hard to repair without removing the entire length of trim. Instead, consider adding a second trim to cover the damaged area.

Lay a length of ribbon over damaged trim and stitch along both edges to secure it.

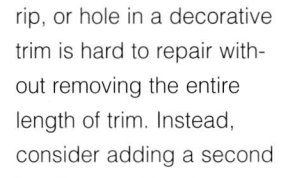
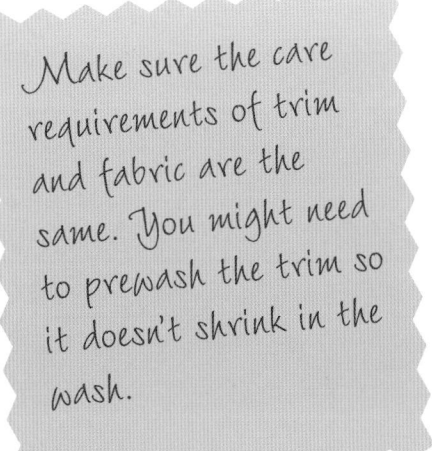

Make sure the care requirements of trim and fabric are the same. You might need to prewash the trim so it doesn't shrink in the wash.

about closures

When a plain white button falls off your favorite shirt, it doesn't mean you have to put a plain white button back on. Just because the snaps keep popping open on your son's pants, you don't have to toss them into the rag bag. And if the zipper feels lumpy on your duvet cover, you don't have to toss off the bedcovers.

There are many kinds of closures—buttons, snaps, hooks and eyes, zippers, hook-and-loop tape, and drawstrings, to name a few. Closures help you open and close your clothing, bags, and other fabric items. When they work, you hardly notice them. When they break or fall off, you notice!

It's easy to replace exactly what was there—but it's also easy to change the fastener to something more interesting, decorative, or effective if you prefer.

There are two types of situations that require closures, and each requires different types. Once you know that, you can get as creative as you want when it's time to replace or mend.

overlapping edges: Choose buttons, snaps, hooks and eyes, or hook-and-loop tape (also known by its trade name, Velcro).

abutting edges: Opt for zippers, decorative and functional hooks and eyes, and drawstrings.

- Buttons are like miniature works of art. You only need to be sure that the new button fits through the original buttonhole (if you're using the button-holes), and that the weight of the button is compatible with the weight of the fabric.

- Rough and textured buttons are easier to grasp if you have special needs or arthritic fingers.

- Replace snaps and hooks and eyes with small squares or circles of hook-and-loop tape, which is easier to manipulate.

- If you don't like the bulk and the ripping sound of hook-and-loop tape, sew on snaps or hooks and eyes instead.

- Replace a zipper closing with multiple tie closures, evenly spaced across the opening.

- Sew-on snaps are not strong enough to hold overlapping edges in high-stress areas. Substitute hook-and-loop tape or gripper snaps.

- Position the loop-shaped eye of a hook and eye set so that it extends beyond the fabric edge—for a neat, secure, but unobtrusive finish at the top of a zipper or in lingerie and bridal wear.

choosing replacement buttons

If a button falls off, just sew it back on the same spot (see page 45). If you lose a button, you have a few options. Start by identifying the style you need: sew-through (flat, with two or four holes), or shank (raised up on a neck or small loop).

If you decide to simply buy a replacement button, take the garment with you to the store to shop for a match. As long as you buy the same size and style, it will fit through the buttonhole. If you can't find the same button, consider replacing all the buttons so they match.

- Check inside the garment along the side seams for an extra button supplied by the manufacturer.

- Remove a button from the lower edge of the garment, especially if it's a shirt that you tuck in. Replace the lower button with any button of similar size. You can also "borrow" buttons from inside waistbands and substitute same-size buttons there.

- Replace the top button on a garment with a unique, antique, or jeweled button, and use the top button to replace the one you've lost.

- Remove a button from a shirt cuff and roll the cuffs instead of buttoning them.

- To camouflage the mismatched button, change a couple of the other buttons, too, to create a decorative "mix and match" style of closure.

- Cover all the buttons with decorative button covers (sold in craft, fabric, and specialty stores and catalogues) to hide the fact that your replacement button isn't a match.

- Buy a fabric-covered button kit and make matching fabric-covered buttons with small pieces of fabric cut from the hem or facing of the garment. Instructions are included in the kit.

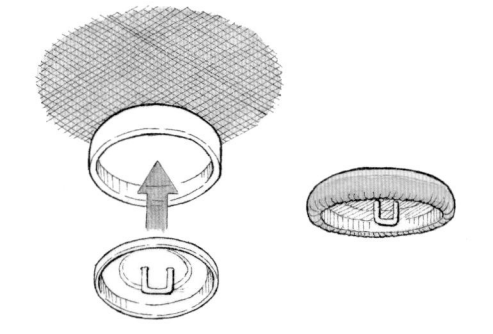

Keep a button box or jar filled with assorted buttons. Remove any wonderful buttons — and plain white shirt buttons, too — from clothes and other items that you're discarding.

sewing on buttons

Nothing is easier than sewing on a button. Just thread a needle. Work with a double strand of thread, about 20" (50.7 cm) long. For lightweight fabrics, use all-purpose thread. Heavy-duty thread or buttonhole twist, a special heavyweight thread, is great for heavier fabrics.

Flat Button

(for lightweight fabrics and nonfunctioning buttons)

Thread the needle and knot the ends together. Bring the needle up from the wrong side of the fabric and through one hole of the button. Bring it back down through the opposite hole and the fabric.

Repeat several times. If there are four holes, stitch through the other two holes the same way.

Knot the thread on the wrong side of the garment.

Shank Button

(for medium- to heavyweight fabrics)

Thread the needle and knot the ends. Position the button with the shank perpendicular to the fabric.

Bring the needle up from the wrong side of the fabric, through the hole in the shank, and back down through the fabric. Sew several stitches through the shank and fabric.

Take two or three tiny stitches on the wrong side of the fabric to secure. Knot the ends.

Flat Button with Thread Shank

(for medium- to heavyweight fabrics)

Thread the needle and knot the ends. Bring the needle up from the wrong side of the fabric and insert it through one hole of the button.

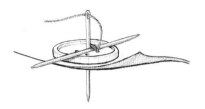

Lay a toothpick across the top of the button. Bring the needle down through the opposite hole, over the toothpick. Take about six stitches. If there are four holes, do the same for the other two holes.

Remove the toothpick and lift the button away from the fabric. Bring the needle out between the button and the fabric surface. Wind the thread around the stitches to create a thread shank.

Take two or three tiny stitches on the wrong side of the fabric to secure and knot the ends.

reinforcing buttons

Buttons pop off for many reasons. If a garment has gotten a little snug, sew the new button a little closer to the edge. If the button is at a stress point, such as the bust or waist, sew a backer button (any small, flat button) to the inside of the garment, behind the fashion button. You can also add backer buttons to closures on heavy fabrics.

Adding a Backer Button

sew-through buttons: Choose a backer button with the same number of holes as the fashion button. Line up the holes and sew on both buttons at the same time.

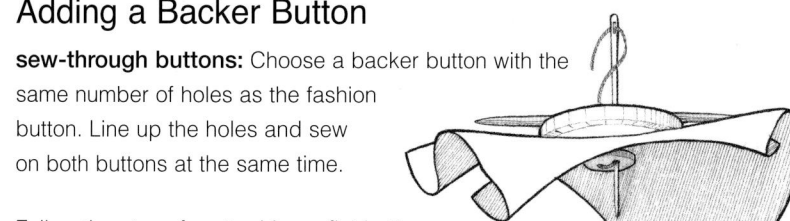

Follow the steps for attaching a flat button with a thread shank (see page 45). If you have a hard time holding both buttons in place, stick a pin through one set of holes while you sew the other set.

shank buttons: Choose a backer button that has two holes. Position the button on the wrong side of the fabric and sew two small stitches through it. Bring the needle to the right side and through the hole in the button shank, as shown in the drawing.

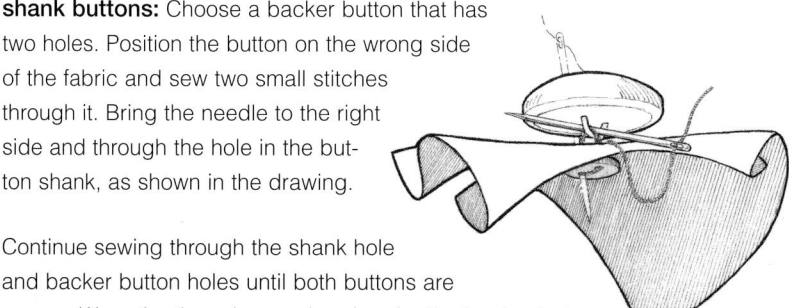

Continue sewing through the shank hole and backer button holes until both buttons are secure. Wrap the thread around and under the backer button and make a knot.

Sewing an Interior Button

It takes a little extra care to sew buttons to the inside of the garment or item—because you don't want the stitches to show on the right side of the fabric. So, as you stitch, do not bring the needle through the fabric. Instead, just pick up a couple of fabric threads on the wrong side with each stitch.

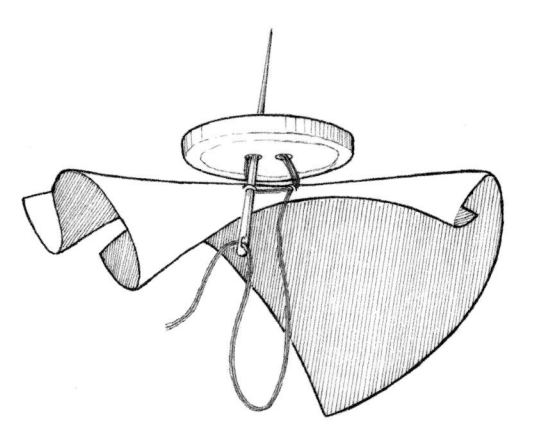

When you're working on a lightweight fabric, sew a small patch of fabric or seam binding behind the button instead of a backer button.

multiple buttons and fabric mends

Whether you're faced with a lot of buttons to sew on, or a nasty fabric tear under a button, there's an easy way to approach the task.

Attaching Buttons by Machine

When you need to attach several sew-through buttons, you might want to use your sewing machine. Attach a button-sewing presser foot (check your manual).

1   Set the machine for a zigzag stitch, with the stitch length at zero.

2   Place the button under the button presser foot, with one hole under the needle. If you need to create a thread shank (a shank makes it easier to button garments made from heavy fabrics), lay a toothpick on top of the button.

3   Adjust the stitch width so the needle goes in and out of the two holes with each stitch. Take several stitches.

4   If the button has four holes, stitch the first two holes. Raise the needle and presser foot and slide the button so the needle goes through the remaining holes. Pull the top thread to the wrong side and knot.

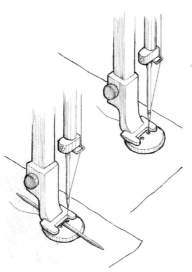

Repairing Torn Fabric

Sometimes, the fabric under a button weakens or tears. You'll need to reinforce the fabric before resewing the button.

1   Cut off any loose threads around the hole

2   Cut a small patch of fabric, backed with fusible web, or fusible mending tape into a circle or oval that is a little larger than the hole.

3   If there is a facing in the item, insert the patch between the facing and the outer fabric. If there is no facing, place the patch on the wrong side of the fabric. To fuse the patch, follow the manufacturer's instructions.

4   Stitch over and across the patch. The stitches should extend slightly beyond the edge of the patch and be invisible on the right side of the fabric. Sew the button, stitching through the patch and creating a thread shank (see page 45).

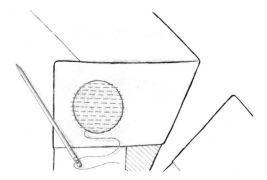

replacing hook fasteners

Hooks and eyes and hook-and-loop tape are simple and unobtrusive fasteners. They keep your garments securely closed without adding bulk. When they fall off, you soon realize how important they are. Note and mark the location of the original fasteners before replacing them.

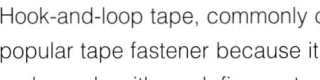

Hooks and Eyes

Hooks and eyes are usually found at the top of a zipper and on fur garments. This two-part fastener comes in several shapes and sizes and is easy to replace.

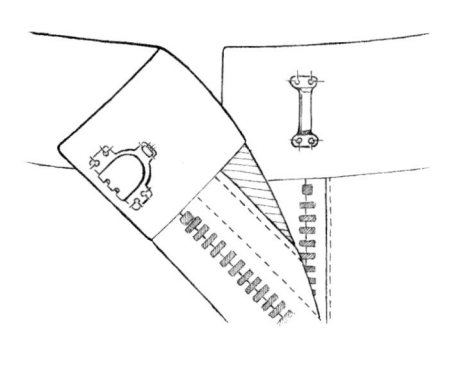

1 Sew the hook section on the underside of the overlap about 1/8" (3 mm) from the edge. Take four or five small, straight stitches around each hole, picking up only one or two threads of fabric so the stitches don't show on the right side.

2 Stitch two or three stitches across and under the hook to keep it flat. Secure the stitching with several small backstitches and a knot buried under the thread.

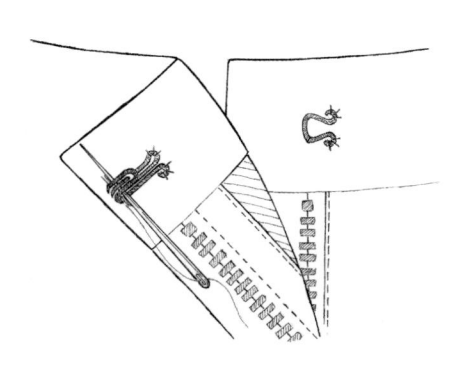

3 Position the eye in place, either so the fabric overlaps or so the edges meet (for example, at the top of a centered zipper), and stitch around the holes as in step 1.

4 If the eye extends beyond the fabric edge, take two small stitches on each side to better secure it. Take several backstitches on the wrong side and knot the thread.

Hook-and-Loop Tape

Hook-and-loop tape, commonly called Velcro, is a popular tape fastener because it's easy for children and people with weak fingers to manipulate. It's also easy to topstitch in place.

If the stitching breaks, just restitch around the edges. If you need to replace the tape, remove the two halves with a seam ripper and replace with new pieces. You can sew them on by hand, but its easier—and more durable—to machine-sew them.

replacing snaps

A snap that keeps popping open doesn't do much good. It just needs to be replaced. Traditional ball-and-socket snaps are great for overlapping edges that aren't subject to a lot of strain. You'll find snap tape on babies' clothing and some home décor items.

If one side of a gripper snap falls off or is torn off, you'll have to replace both elements to ensure the right fit. Cut around the snap pieces, then patch the holes (see page 30). Following the instructions in the snap and applicator package, apply new ball and socket pieces over the patches.

Ball-and-Socket Snaps

1 Attach the ball section to the wrong side of the overlap, close to the edge. Take three or four straight stitches through each hole. Take care that your stitches don't go through to the right side of the garment. Secure with two or three backstitches and a knot near the snap.

2 Position the socket so it aligns with the ball section and sew it to the fabric as in step 1. Your stitches can go through the fabric because they'll be hidden inside the garment.

Snap Tape

If a single snap on a strip of snap tape stops working, the other snaps will probably keep the garment or item closed. If they don't, however, remove both pieces of snap tape by picking out the stitching that holds it in place.

Pin the two halves of a new tape in place. Double-check that the ball and socket elements align properly. Working with a zipper foot, edge-stitch by machine through all layers of the tape and fabric.

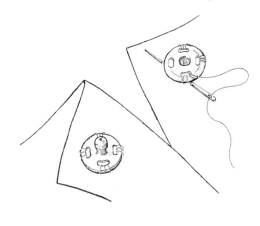

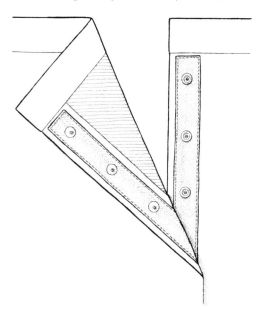

fixing drawstrings

Don't despair if the drawstring in your favorite pants pulls out—it's easy to replace it and to make sure that it doesn't slip out again.

Reinserting a Drawstring

If one end of the drawstring has disappeared into the casing, pull out the entire string. Attach a safety pin to one end and insert it into the casing.

Push and pull the safety pin through the casing and out the opposite opening. Be careful not to pull the unpinned end of the drawstring all the way into the casing. Pull on both ends to even their lengths.

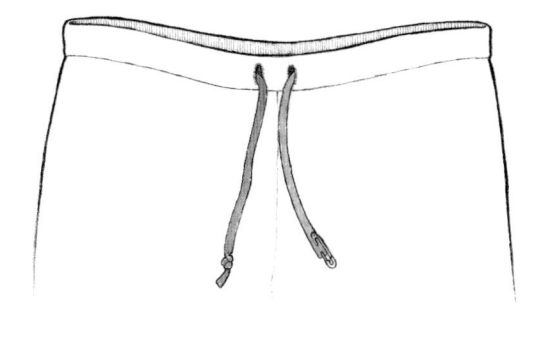

Keeping the Ends in Sight

To avoid losing the ends in the casing, make small overhand knots at each end. Or, at each end, sew a button, tassel, or charm that is too large to fit through the casing. You can also simply tie the ends together when you launder the item.

Securing the String

You can stitch the drawstring in place to secure it. Center the string inside the casing, so equal amounts extend from each opening. At the center of the casing, topstitch across the width of the casing and drawstring to secure the string in place.

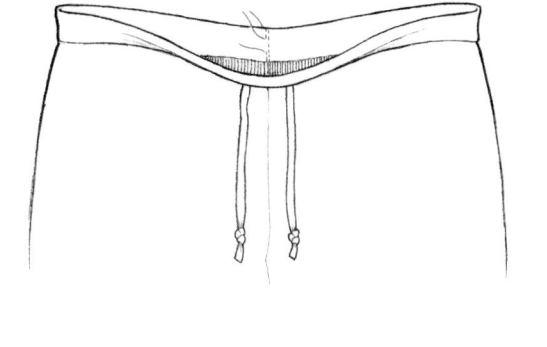

If the fabric around the casing opening is torn, remove the drawstring and darn the area as well as you can without sewing the casing closed.

fixing frayed buttonholes

Repair a buttonhole as soon as you notice that it's fraying. You want to fix it before more of the stitches tear or the fabric stretches.

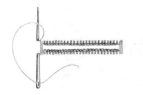

Working by Hand

Thread the needle with a double length of thread that matches the existing thread. Trim away any loose threads to neaten the buttonhole area.

1   Insert the needle to the right of the torn stitches on the wrong side of the fabric. Take two or three backstitches. Pull the needle up through the opening and take enough buttonhole stitches (see page 19) to cover the frayed and torn area.

If the entire buttonhole is weak, stitch over the existing stitches all the way around the buttonhole. Pull the thread firmly, but not too tightly, so that the loops fall exactly on the edge of the buttonhole.

2   Restitch the bar tacks if necessary.

Working by Machine

Before repairing a buttonhole by machine, make a practice row of narrow and short zigzag stitches on scrap fabric. Make sure the stitches resemble the original buttonhole stitches.

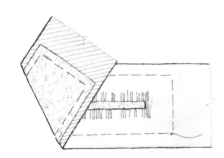

1   Carefully remove the frayed stitches. Baste or fuse a small piece of stabilizer or interfacing around the back of the buttonhole to support the area. Make sure the two buttonhole edges are close together, but not touching.

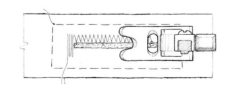

2   On the right side of the fabric, zigzag-stitch over the frayed area, starting and continuing slightly beyond the frayed area.

If the buttonhole is just starting to fray, dab it with Fray Check to keep it from getting any worse.

making a new buttonhole

If a buttonhole is frayed beyond repair, you can easily stitch a new one with the sewing machine. Either use the built-in buttonhole function, if your machine has one, or follow these easy steps to make a bar-tack buttonhole.

Preparing the Buttonhole

1. Working with a seam ripper, remove any remaining buttonhole stitches from the wrong side of the fabric. Pull out the remaining thread bits with a tweezers. Mark the ends (just outside the bar tacks) of the old buttonhole with a fabric-marking pen.

2. Fuse a piece of interfacing or baste tear-away stabilizer to the wrong side of the fabric under the old buttonhole, to hold the opening closed.

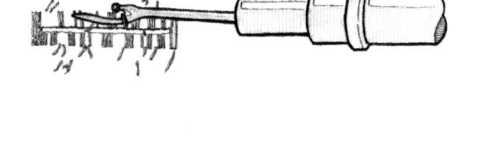

Making a Bar-Tack Buttonhole

1. Attach a zigzag or buttonhole presser foot to your machine. Lower the foot over the center marking. Set the machine for a very short stitch length and stitch three or four wide zigzag stitches across the end to form the first bar tack.

2. Reduce the stitch width. Zigzag-stitch down one side of the buttonhole opening to the other marked end.

3. Reset for the wider zigzag stitch setting and sew the remaining bar tack.

4. Adjust the machine setting for a narrow zigzag stitch. Turn the fabric around. Stitch the opposite side, back to the first bar tack. Make one or two small stitches to secure threads.

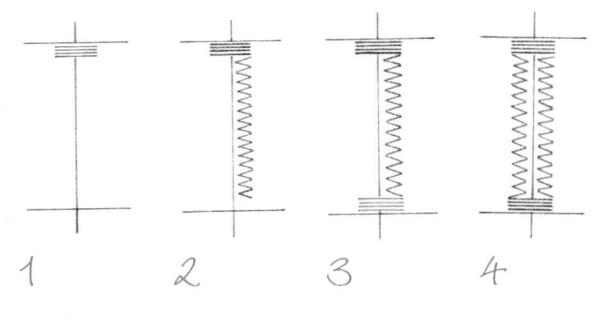

Cutting Open the Buttonhole

Be careful not to cut through the bar tacks. Insert straight pins just inside the bar tack at each end of the buttonhole. With sharp scissors or a seam ripper, carefully cut along the center of the buttonhole between the rows of zigzag stitches.

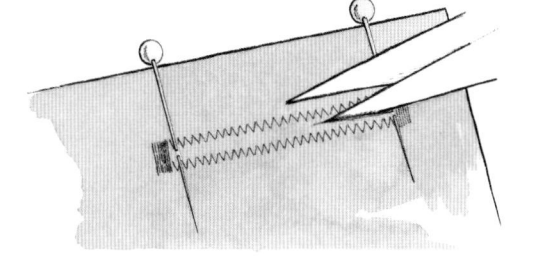

quick fixes
for buttonholes

Buttonholes that are subject to a lot of stress—for example, at a waist-band or bust line—can easily tear, along with the fabric around them. Luckily, buttonholes with tears, stretched fabric, and loose stitching can be repaired with a quick fix.

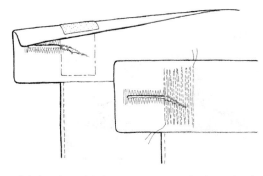

torn fabric: If the fabric tears at one or both ends of the buttonhole, mend it by fusing a fabric patch to the wrong side to hold the torn edges together. Fuse a patch of similar color and weight as the fabric.

Darn over the tear (see page 28). Restitch the torn buttonhole stitches, following the instructions on page 51.

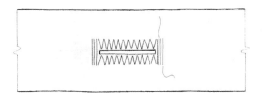

torn bar tack: To strengthen a bar tack, sew several wide, closely spaced zigzag stitches over the ripped stitches.

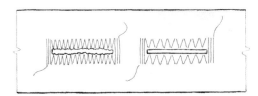

rippled buttonholes: If the buttonhole stitching is too dense in a knit or stretch fabric, the buttonhole will ripple. Stabilize the area with a scrap of fusible interfacing and pull out the old buttonhole with a seam ripper. Restitch a new buttonhole using a longer zigzag stitch.

stretched-out buttonholes: Pin the buttonhole closed. Stabilize the area by fusing two narrow strips of interfacing as close as possible to each side of the buttonhole on the wrong side of the fabric.

gaping buttonholes: On the wrong side of the fabric, run a heavy thread under one row of stitches, around one end, and back up under the opposite row. Pull the thread slightly to straighten the buttonhole. Knot the ends and hide the knot under the stitches.

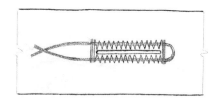

Shorten a buttonhole that keeps popping open by sewing several wide zigzag stitches inside one or both bar tacks.

creative buttonhole repairs

Want a more creative fix for torn or frayed buttonholes? You have several choices. Color-blocked patches, ribbon trim, fabric bands, and even purchased appliqués are great ways to cover damaged or torn buttonholes. The challenge is to make the repair look like part of the design.

Fabric ties

Before applying a new closure, remove the buttons. Pin any facing off to the side so you don't catch it in the repair. Fuse a small piece of interfacing to the wrong side of the fabric to permanently close the buttonholes or hand-stitch them closed.

fabric ties: Sew your own ties from fabric or decorative trim or cording. Cut two lengths, making sure they are long enough to tie in a knot or bow. Trim later. Topstitch one tie so it covers the buttonhole. Topstitch the other to the right of the original button location. Knot the ties to close.

flat trim: Fuse or baste a length of flat ribbon or trim along both edges of the opening, covering the but-

tonholes and button locations. Fold the ends of the trim under to conceal them. Edge-stitch by machine to secure the trim in place.

fabric patches and decorative closures: Cut fabric or leather patches to cover the buttonholes. If the patch fabric ravels, fold the edges to the wrong side. Fuse and then topstitch the patches in place. Sew decorative buttons, toggles, or bows over the patches. Sew metal snaps or hooks and eyes on the inside to keep the garment closed.

fabric flower or appliqué: When you have sewn or fused the buttonhole closed, pin a large fabric flower over it, or hand-sew an appliqué in place to cover it. Sew a metal hook and eye on the inside of the opening to securely close the garment.

Flat trim

Decorative closures

Fabric flower

replacing elastic

Elastic is a narrow, flexible, stretchable strip that is either enclosed in a casing or stitched directly onto a garment. Time and many trips through a hot clothes dryer can damage elastic, causing it to stretch and lose recovery (the ability to spring back to size). To replace elastic, measure the width of the existing elastic and replace it with a strip of the same type and size. If you plan to sew the elastic to the garment, cut it slightly shorter because it will stretch while you are stitching.

Applied Elastic

1 With a seam ripper (see page 14), remove the stitches that hold the existing elastic. If you are replacing elastic on a sleeve or pant hem, convert your sewing machine to a free arm to make it easier to sew (check your machine manual). Or, open the seam far enough so you can flatten the area to make it easier to sew.

Divide the area where you will apply the elastic into four equal sections. Mark with pins. Divide and pin-mark the elastic into equal fourths, too. Leave the width of the seam allowance free at both ends of the elastic and the garment section.

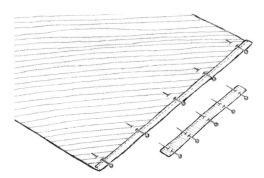

2 Pin the elastic to the wrong side of the garment, matching the quarter markings on the elastic and the fabric. Leave the seam allowances free at each end. Add pins as needed to stretch the elastic across the entire length of fabric. The fabric will gather.

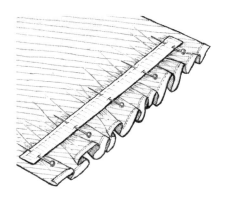

3 Zigzag-stitch the elastic to the fabric, stretching it between the pins. Hold the fabric taut with one hand behind the presser foot and the other hand in front of the foot. Let the feed dogs move the fabric.

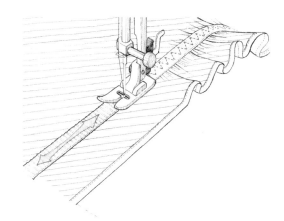

Elastic in a Casing

1 Remove about 1" (2.5 cm) of the casing stitches with a seam ripper (see page 14). Work in an unobtrusive area, such as the side seam, and along the lower edge of the casing.

2 Pull a tiny bit of elastic out of the opening and cut it. With a safety pin, join one of the cut ends to one end of the new elastic. Round off the corners of the new elastic so it moves through the casing more easily.

Pull the unpinned end of the old elastic out of the casing, drawing the new elastic into the casing. Leave the last 2" (5 cm) of the new elastic exposed at each end.

3 Unpin and remove the old elastic from the end of the casing. Make sure the new elastic lies flat inside the casing. Overlap and join the ends of the new elastic by hand or zigzag stitch by machine.

4 Stretch the elastic to pull the ends into the casing and distribute any gathers in the fabric. Edge-stitch or hand-stitch the opening closed, being careful not to catch the elastic in the stitches.

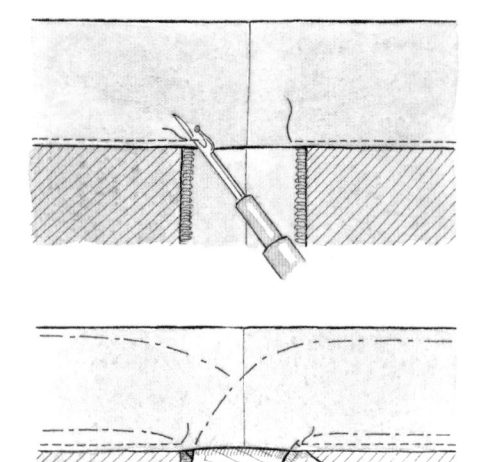

1

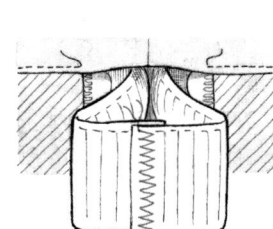

2

3

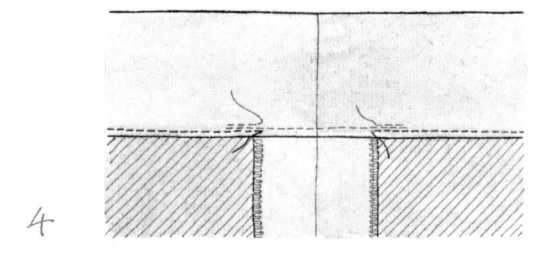

4

To determine how much elastic you need, wrap the new elastic around your body (at waist, wrist, or ankle) and add 1" (2.5 cm) for finishing the ends.

repairing lining

A lining adds longevity to an item, but, unfortunately, it often wears out before the fashion fabric does. It's easy to patch a small damaged or worn area, but if the lining is visible, it's best to replace the entire piece or panel. In tailored garments—jackets and coats, for example—it's sometimes easier to just cut away the damaged lining and live without it.

Patch garment linings with fabric that matches the existing lining in color, weight, and fiber content. Patch home-décor items with muslin or cotton sateen. Preshrink the lining fabric.

patching lining: To patch a small or inconspicuous area, cut a patch that is slightly larger all around than the worn area. Press 1/4" (6 mm) of the patch under on all sides. Pin the patch in place. Edge-stitch the patch by machine or slip stitch it by hand.

mending lining: To mend a torn lining, pin the edges of the tear with right sides together and stitch it closed. Machine-stitch from the wrong side if you can. If you can't, hand-stitch from the right side.

removing lining: If the lining is badly torn, replace or remove it. The simplest way to remove lining is to cut it as close as possible to the seams—although you'll leave a few threads. If the inside of the item is visible, you might prefer to open the seams to remove the lining.

Working with a seam ripper, open the seams that secure the lining. Remove the entire lining, then resew the seams. It's often easier to sew these seams by hand because they can be difficult to reach by machine.

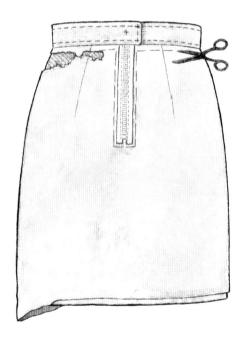

guidelines for adjusting fit

If you're one of the few people who can buy clothing right off the rack, congratulations! The rest of us usually need to make some small (or large) fitting adjustments. If you've got a couple of impulse purchases still hanging in the back of your closet or you just can't seem to fit into some of those old favorites—a quick tuck or a loosened seam might be just what your wardrobe needs!

Fitting Tips

- Launder the item first. If it's new, it might shrink in the wash. If not, you want to remove any dirt so you don't press it into the fabric as you are making the alteration.

- Try on the garment while wearing the proper undergarments and accessories.

- Bear in mind that it's easier to make something smaller than larger.

- Pin the alterations from the right side of the garment. Double-check to make sure that you like how the alteration looks before you begin sewing.

- Mark the pin locations on the inside of the garment and baste along the markings.

- Try on the garment again after basting to make sure the alteration is still correct.

- Save the altering of tailored garments, eveningwear, and specialty fabrics for the tailor. Narrowing pant legs, shortening spaghetti straps, and letting out a seam are quick fixes that can even be done by hand.

- Press often as you sew for a crisp, precise result.

- Make some notes about the garment, so you can match the thread, stitch length, and construction methods.

- Work with a seam ripper to take out any seams that need adjustment (see page 14).

- Press out all crease lines.

- Plan to conceal any crease lines that can't be eliminated by pressing.

- Press with a damp press cloth to close visible holes left after ripping out a seam.

It's hard to see the back of a garment when you're wearing it, so enlist the help of a friend to pin and mark adjustments— and possibly offer an opinion on the fit.

when it's too tight

When a garment is too tight, the first and easiest option is to let out a side seam or another vertical seam. The standard seam allowance is ⁵/₈" (1.5 cm), but in manufactured garments the allowance is often trimmed. Usually you can gain ¹/₂" (1.3 cm) at each seam, which might be just enough to make the garment fit more comfortably.

adjusting at the seams:
Measure from the original seam line to the edge of the fabric to see how much extra fabric you gain.

You'll need a minimum of ¹/₄" (6 mm) for a new seam allowance. If there's ¹/₂" (1.3 cm) or more beyond that, you'll be able to increase the garment by at least ¹/₂" (1.3 cm) per seam.

Side seams, sleeves, and armholes are the easiest seams to let out. Pull out the seam with the seam ripper. Press both sides and restitch close to, but not on, the raw edge.

widening seam allowances:
If the seam allowances are too narrow to allow much extra width, sew a strip of twill tape or seam tape to the edges. Press. Resew the seam very close to the tape extensions, without catching them in the seam.

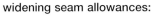

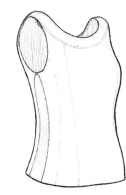

adding a gusset: A gusset is a piece of fabric of any shape that is inserted into a seam to allow greater ease of movement. A gusset is usually added at side seams and is made of matching fabric (if possible), but you can also use contrast fabric or trim.

To make a gusset, rip out the seams that are too tight. Try on the garment and measure the gap in the open seams. Cut a gusset large enough to fill the gap. Pin the gusset at the seams.

Try on the garment again and adjust the gusset to ensure a comfortable fit. Sew the new seams.

closing side-seam pockets:
If pockets on the side seams gape open, turn the garment inside out and sew the pockets closed. Cut away the pocket bags inside the garment and zigzag the edges.

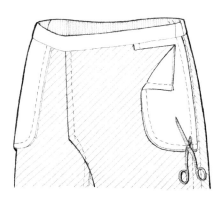

when it's too loose

Changing an entire garment to a smaller size is a job best left to a tailor. Otherwise, to fix a loose fit, you can just take in any one of a number of seams. The biggest challenge you face when taking in seams is preserving the silhouette and drape of the garment.

Taking in Straight Seams

Pin the alteration and try on the garment. Baste the new seams and try on the garment again. When you are satisfied with the the fit, stitch the seams with a standard stitch length. Trim the excess fabric. Press and zigzag the edges. Whenever possible, distribute the adjustment by altering two or more seams a little, rather than one seam a lot.

Taking in a Pant Waistband at Center Back

1 Try on the pants and have a friend pin the excess fabric at the center back seam.

2 With a fabric-marking pen or tailor's chalk, mark the pin locations to create a new stitching line inside the pants.

Remove the belt loop and waistband facing and open the center back seam with a seam ripper. If there is no seam, cut the existing waistband at center back.

3 Stitch the new center back seam, extending it through the waistband facing. Trim the excess fabric, if desired. Press the seam allowances open and resew the facing. Reattach the belt loop.

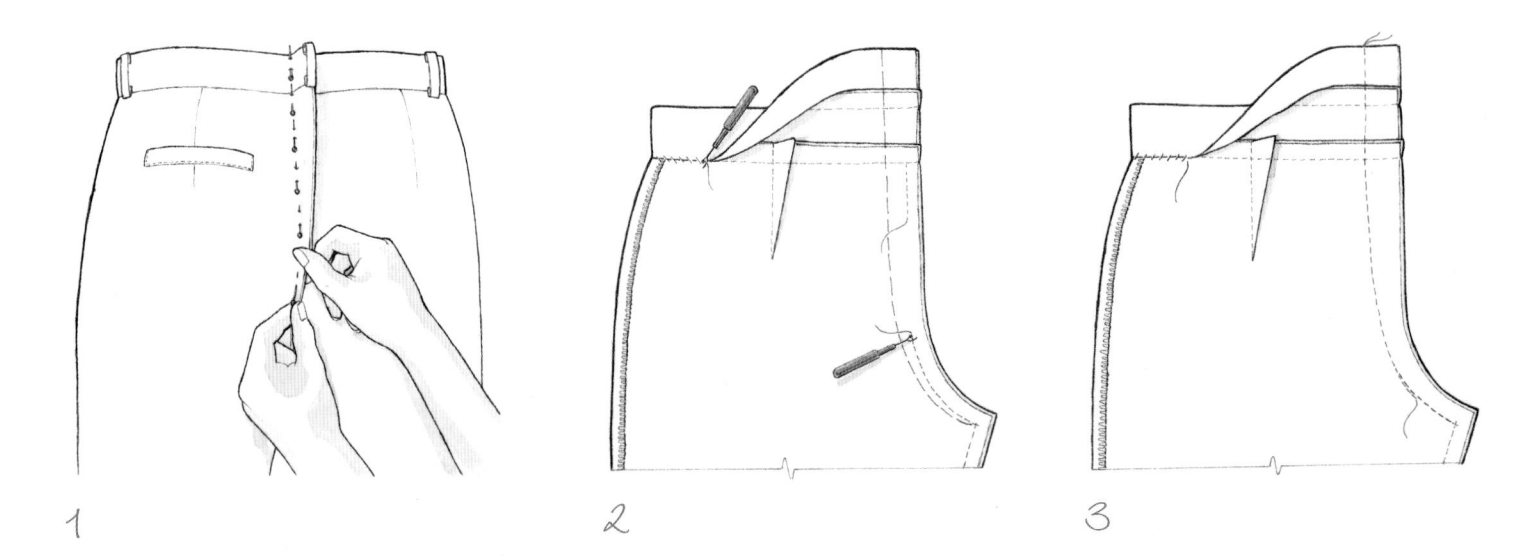

1   2   3

when it's too wide

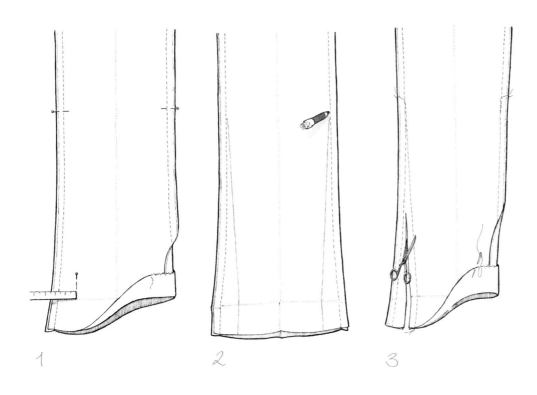

1

2

3

Narrowing Pant Legs

1 Try on the pants and pin them to see how much fullness you want to remove. Measure the total amount. Rip out the hem with a seam ripper (see page 14). Press.

On the hem crease line, measure and mark half the total desired amount from each seam. Make equal adjustments to the outer and inner seam so that the pants to hang straight.

2 With tailor's chalk or a fabric-marking pen, mark the new seam lines, starting at or just above the knee and continuing to the hem.

3 Stitch the new seams. Adjust the depth of the hem allowance to accommodate the new pant-leg width. Trim the seam allowance and zigzag the new edges. Rehem the pants (see pages 65 and 66).

Turn a blousy shirt into a more tailored style by sewing a series of vertical darts or tucks around the torso.

stretched and frayed necklines

Necklines and collars receive a lot of wear and tear—and they often look worn before the rest of the garment does. To add years to the life of a good-quality sweater or shirt, just fix the collar or neckline.

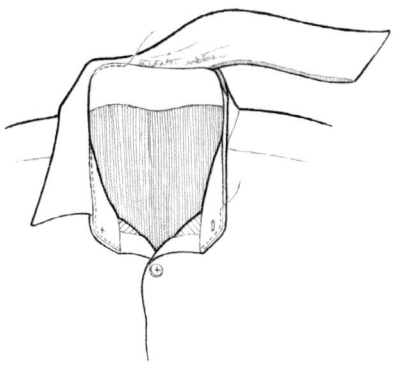

ribbing on sweaters: Thread a long needle with elastic thread and knot the end. Working from the wrong side of the sweater, sew small running stitches from one rib to the next all around the neckline (this works for cuffs and hems, too). Make sure the stitches aren't visible on the right side.

Repeat with two or three additional rows of running stitches, spaced about 1/2" (1.3 cm) apart. Steam the elastic thread to shrink it slightly.

off-the-shoulder necklines: To form a casing, hand-sew ribbon or seam tape on the wrong side of the garment just below the finished neck edge. Insert narrow elastic through the casing with a safety pin.

Adjust the elastic so it doesn't gather the neck edge but instead holds the edge of the garment close to the body. Hand-sew the elastic ends together and tuck them inside the casing.

shirt collars: When the roll line of a collar becomes worn, turn the collar to reveal the fresh underside. With a seam ripper (page 14), remove the collar from its stand.

Turn the collar over, insert the raw edges into the collar stand, and edge-stitch them in place. (You can make the same repair with shirt cuffs, too.)

You can convert a traditional shirt collar to a band collar. Just unstitch the collar stand to release the collar, then edge-stitch the stand to close it.

fixing a torn hem

One of the most common repair jobs is fixing a torn or loose hem. It's also one of the easiest. If you don't want or need to change the length of the item, simply restitch the loose section, exactly as it was originally stitched.

Hand-Stitching

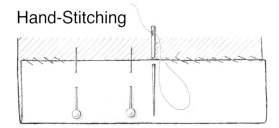

For the most invisible repair, restitch hems by hand. Press the hem and pin it back in place. Use any hand-hemming stitch shown on page 65 that resembles the original stitching and doesn't show on the right side of the fabric.

Fusing

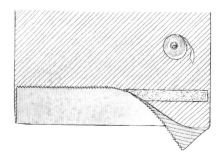

Keep fusible web or fusible hemming tape on hand for quick, no-sew hem repairs. Fusibles are best suited to light- to medium-weight woven fabrics and straight hems.

Insert a 1/2" (1.3 cm)-wide strip of fusible web between the hem allowance and the garment along the hemline and press to secure (see page 22).

Temporary Fixes

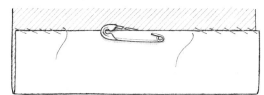

For a quick, emergency fix, hold a torn hem in place with double-sided tape or duct tape. The repair will last at least a few hours. Or safety-pin the hem at the side seams and intermittently across the ripped area—but try not to pin through to the right side so you keep the repair invisible.

If you're in a real bind, you can also staple the hem allowance to the side seams of the garment. Join the hem allowance only to the seam allowances inside to avoid damaging the outer fabric of the garment.

Machine-Stitching

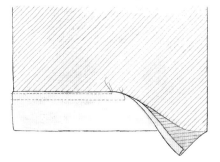

If the original hem of the garment was machine-sewn, repair it by machine, duplicating the original stitching as closely as possible. Topstitch knits by machine with a stretch stitch. If there are two rows of topstitching, you can work with a twin needle (see page 10) to create perfectly parallel stitching.

repairing hems by hand

To sew hems by hand, thread the needle with a single strand of matching color thread and knot one end (see page 17). Begin sewing about 1/2" (1.3 cm) before the beginning of the torn stitches. Don't pull the stitches too tightly. To secure the new stitching, take a small backstitch in the hem allowance every 4" to 6" (10 to 15 cm).

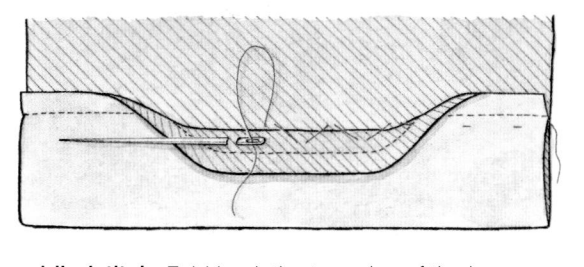

blindstitch: Fold back the top edge of the hem. Take a tiny stitch in and out of the garment fabric, catching only one or two threads on the surface. Take the next stitch 1/4" (6 mm) away within the allowance. Repeat, keeping stitches small and 1/4" (6 mm) apart. The stitches will be hidden between the layers of fabric.

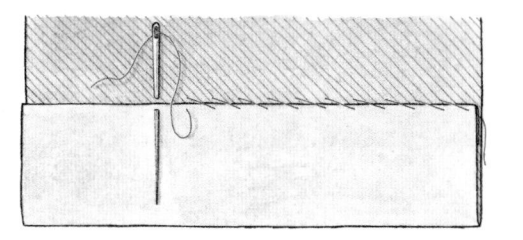

hemming stitch: Take a tiny stitch in and out of the garment, catching only one or two threads of the garment. Then bring the needle through the edge of the hem. Repeat, evenly spacing and slanting the stitches.

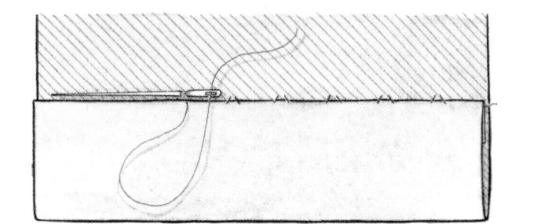

slip stitch: Insert the needle inside the fabric fold of the hem allowance and bring it out through the folded edge about 1/4" (6 mm) away. Insert the needle in and out of the garment fabric, catching only one or two threads of the fabric. Repeat, alternating from the hem allowance edge to the garment with each stitch.

Press only the bottom edge of the hem so the thickness of the fabric layers at the top of the hem won't leave an imprint on the front of the garment.

repairing hems by machine

Some hems are perfectly suited to a quick mend by machine. It's always easiest to copy the hemming method that was originally done, especially if only part of the hem has ripped out.

machine topstitch: You'll often find a machine-topstitched hem on casual clothing, curtains, draperies, and outdoor gear. Fold and pin the torn hem in place.

Topstitch on the right side so that the stitches are the same width from the edge as the existing hem stitches. Start and stop stitching 1/2" (1.3 cm) before and beyond the ripped section.

If the item has a double row of topstitching, stitch the first row of topstitching the same width from the edge as the intact stitches. Then use the toe of the presser foot as a guide for the second row, as shown in the drawing. Stitch slowly to keep the two rows parallel.

machine-stitched narrow hem: Narrow hems are usually found on sheer, silky, and bias-cut garments. Most narrow hems are folded twice, to enclose the raw edge, and then stitched.

Before stitching, you need to repress the hem as it was originally pressed, to make sure it's even and that the raw edge is caught in the hem. Machine-stitch close to the inside fold.

If the fabric is torn near the hem, you might need to trim off the entire bottom of the garment, just above the tear, and re-sew the hem. For a new narrow hem, press under 1/2" (1.3 cm) and then 1/2" (1.3 cm) again. Machine-stitch close to the inside fold.

machine blindstitch: Install the blindstitch presser foot. Refer to your manual for instructions for your machine. Place the hem allowance face down on the machine bed and fold back the rest of the fabric. Allow about 1/4" (6 mm) of the hem edge to extend under the presser foot, aligning the soft fold against the guide in the foot.

Stitch along the hem, close to the fold, catching only one or two threads of the garment with each left-hand stitch. Open the hem and press it flat.

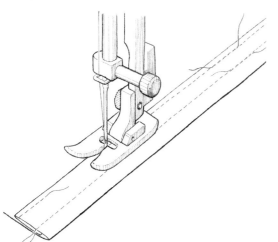
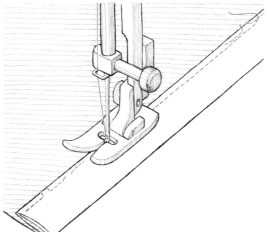
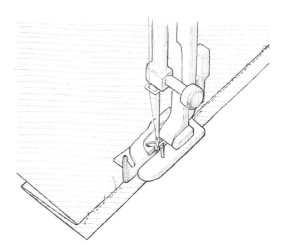

making a simple hem

If you don't have a sewing buddy who can mark your hem, you can purchase a floor-standing chalk hem marker. This handy device marks the hemline an even height from the floor.

You can shorten any type of garment. You might want to hide a frayed edge or update the look of a favorite skirt or coat. Items with straight hems are the easiest to shorten, but you can rehem pleated, tapered, flared, and cuffed garments, with just a couple of extra steps. With these same, simple techniques, you can make a change that is barely perceptible or one that will alter the entire look.

Marking for a Hem

Begin by removing the stitching in the original hem. Put on the garment, while wearing the appropriate undergarments and footwear. Enlist the help of a friend to mark the hem with chalk or pins so that it is an even height from the floor all the way around the bottom of the garment.

Stand in place and ask your helper to move around you, measuring with a yardstick while marking. Pin up the hem along the marked line and double-check to be sure you like the new length.

Mark a new hem on a curtain or other home accessory by placing the item in position and pin-marking its desired length with a yardstick. Measure from the floor to make sure the hem is even.

Adding a Hem Allowance

When you are satisfied with the new hemline, mark a cutting line, allowing extra for the desired hem allowance below the new hemline. The standard hem allowance for a straight garment is up to 3" (7.5 cm) wide. For a flared garment, it is 1/2" to 2" (1.3 to 5 cm) wide. (Allowances for hand-sewn hems are usually wider than allowances for machine-sewn hems.)

The hems on curtains, draperies, table, and bed linens vary—from a 6" (15 cm) double-fold hem to a 1/2" (1.3 cm) double-fold hem. After adding the hem allowance cut the excess fabric from the item, leaving 1/4" to 1/2" (6 mm to 1.3 cm) for a clean-finished edge.

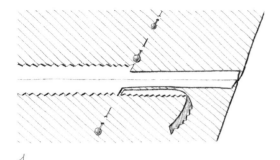

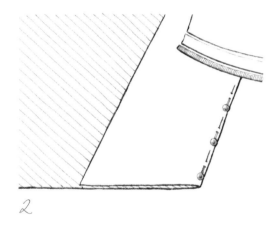

Finishing the Cut Edge

- Clean-finishing the cut edge of the hem allowance prevents fraying and raveling, so your new hem lasts longer and looks neater from the inside. There are many ways to clean-finish the cut fabric edge before hemming.

- Turn under ¼" (6 mm) of the hem to the wrong side. Press and machine-stitch close to the fold.

- Machine-zigzag along the raw edge.

- Edge-stitch a length of seam binding or hem tape to the right side of the garment's edge, overlapping short ends.

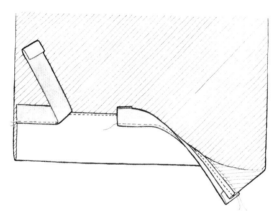

Preparing to Hem

For the neatest, smoothest hem, follow these prep steps, then sew. It's worth the time to press, clean-finish, and ease the hem allowance before stitching the hem—a puckered, bulky hemline can ruin an otherwise gorgeous garment.

1. Trim the garment's seam allowances in the area below the marked hemline to reduce bulk.

2. Fold up the hem along the pin-marked line and press.

3. If the garment is wider at the raw edge than at the hem fold line, stitch 1/4" (6 mm) from the raw edge with a long machine stitch. Pull up the bobbin thread every few inches to gather the fullness very slightly.

   Stitch a new hem by hand or machine, as described on pages 64–65.

shortening with fabric tucks

Fabric tucks are a creative and effective way to shorten an item without cutting fabric or removing the existing hem. This quick fix is especially useful when shortening clothes for children—tucks are quickly and easily reversible as children grow taller.

Hidden Tucks

To shorten cuffed pants or shirts—without removing the cuff—simply sew a tuck at the cuff's seam line.

to shorten pants, fold and pin the pant legs with an even tuck of fabric on the inside of the pant leg, hidden behind the cuff. Try on the pants. If they're okay, sew the tucks in place, making sure the seam is below the upper edge of the cuff. Press the tuck toward the hem.

to shorten a cuffed shirtsleeve, fold the extra length at the cuff seam, so that the fold of fabric extends behind the cuff, inside the garment. Stitch the tuck, close to or directly over the cuff seam.

If the tuck is bulky, cut away the excess fabric close to the stitching, then zigzag-stitch the cut edges.

Decorative Tucks

Shorten garments or curtains with horizontal tucks positioned near the hem edge. Make one or more tucks to remove the desired amount of length.

Working with a fabric-marking pen on the wrong side of the fabric, mark two parallel tuck fold lines for each tuck, separated by twice the desired finished depth of the tuck. Pin the tucks along these lines, then sew them in place with a machine straight stitch. Press the tuck folds toward the hem.

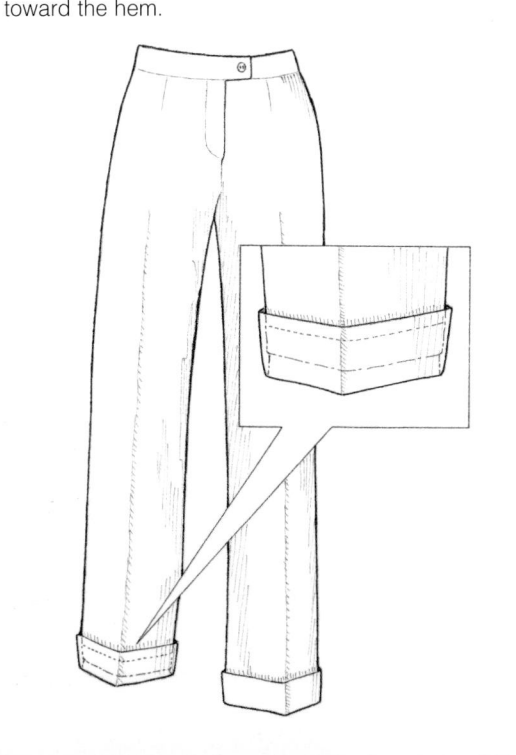

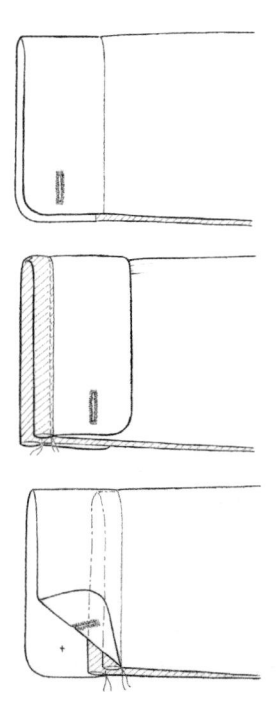

hemming
decorative edges

Fancy border prints or embroidered hemlines call for special hemming treatment. You can't just fold up the bottom. Instead, subtract length farther up the seam.

shortening above the embellished section: Decide how much shorter you want the item to be. Mark one cutting line 1/2" (1.3 cm) above the top edge of the border. Mark a second line the amount you want to shorten the item (and subtract 1/2" [1.3 cm] for the seam allowance). Cut along the marked lines, as shown in the drawing.

With right sides together and cut edges aligned, place the border section on the new hemline. Join the two pieces with a 1/2" (1.3 cm) seam allowance. Press the seam allowances toward the hem and zigzag the edges.

shortening at the waist: Decide how much shorter you want the item to be and determine how many inches you need to remove. Measure down the garment from the waist and mark the amount to be shortened (and subtract 1/2" [1.3 cm] for the seam allowance).

Remove the waistband (and zipper if there is one) with a seam ripper. Cut the fabric at the marked line. Replace the zipper, resew the darts, and reattach the waistband at the new top edge of the garment.

If you shorten a darted garment at the waist, you don't have to copy the original darts. Put on the garment and pin in custom-fitted darts. Stitch them in place, and resew the waistband.

shortening tapered or flared garments

Have you ever tried to shorten a flared skirt and found you have cut away all the styling? Or have you ever tried to shorten a tapered pair of pants and found the hem allowance too tight to work with? Sometimes shortening a garment changes its fit, silhouette, and drape. Here's how to handle a variety of shaped hems.

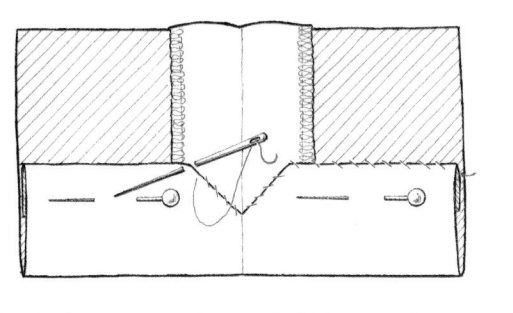

shortening narrow, tapered skirt or pants:
Measure, mark, and prepare the hem, as described on pages 66–77. Open the side seams of the hem allowance with a seam ripper, so you can spread the allowance to fit. When sewing the hem, secure the opened hem allowance to the side seam allowances.

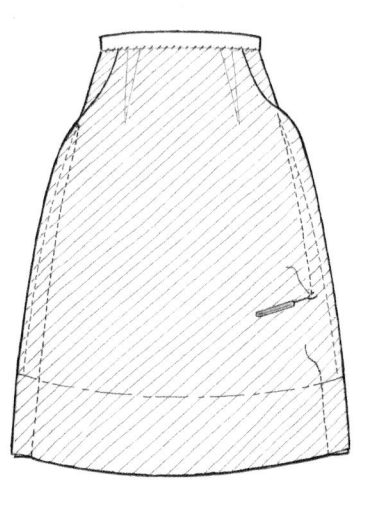

shortening flared pants, skirts, or dresses: You'll change the shape of a flared garment if you shorten it more than 2" (5 cm). Let out the side seams below the hipline to put flare back into the hem area. Work with a seam ripper to open the side seams from the hipline to the hemline.

Draw a new stitching line from the hipline, gradually narrowing the seam allowances to almost nothing at the hemline. Stitch the new side seams and then stitch the flared hem, easing as described in step 3 on page 67.

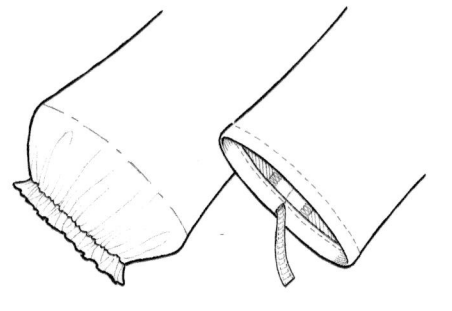

shortening pant legs or sleeves with elastic casing: Open the casing and remove the elastic. Mark the desired new hem length, adding an allowance for the new casing (make the casing the width of the elastic plus 1/4" [6 mm]).

Cut off the excess fabric and fold the casing to the wrong side. Sew the casing in place, stitching close to the cut edge and leaving an opening for inserting the elastic. Insert the elastic from the old casing into the new one (see page 56), then sew the opening closed.

Or you can cut off the elastic casing entirely and simply machine-stitch a narrow hem, but keep in mind that the pants or sleeves will then be much wider at the hem.

lengthening at the hem

Lengthening is a bit more challenging than shortening, but definitely doable. The first and easiest option is to simply remove the stitching, let down the hem allowance, and press it flat. If there isn't enough fabric in the hem allowance, to lengthen as much as you want there are several options.

narrow hemming: If there is enough fabric in the hem allowance to lengthen the item as much as you'd like to, resew the hem with a narrow double-folded hem (see page 65).

If the garment has a cuff, you can narrow the cuff or use the cuff allowance to add length.

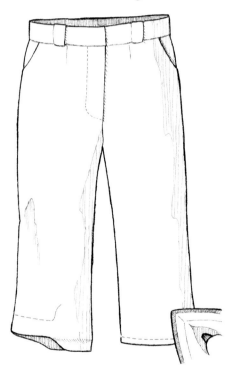

topstitching decorative trim: Attach trim to the lower edge of the unfolded or stitched hem with basting tape, glue, or running stitches (see page 18). Topstitch it in place (see page 21) with one or more rows of stitches—you can use straight or decorative stitches. Make sure the care requirements of the trim match that of the item itself.

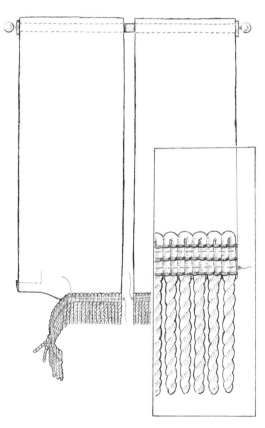

attaching bias binding: You can add length with extra-wide bias binding. Cut the binding so the length equals the hem circumference plus 1" (2.5 cm). Sew the short ends of the binding with right sides together.

Pin one edge of the bias binding to the hem edge with right sides together and raw edges aligned.

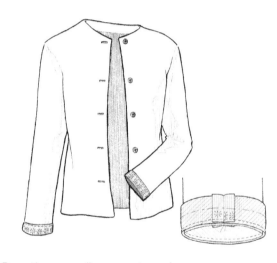

Press the seam allowances toward the binding. Fold the free edge of the tape under to enclose the raw edge and just cover the stitching. Machine- or hand-stitch in place.

lengthening with a facing or ruffle

It's easy to add length by attaching extra fabric at the hem. Open the existing hem, press the crease flat, then add a facing or ruffle. A facing will be invisible, while a ruffle changes the look of an item.

making a faced hem: Cut a hem facing from lining fabric or seam tape. The facing length should equal the hem circumference plus 1" (2.5 cm). The width should be about 2" (5 cm) or the finished width of the seam tape.

For circular hems (as on skirts), sew the short edges of the facing with right sides together, using 1/2" (1.3 cm) seam allowances.

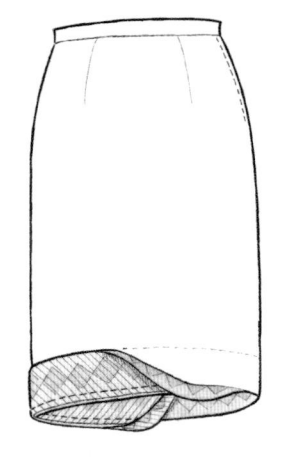

With right sides together, sew the facing to the lower edge of the item. Clean-finish the unstitched facing edge if necessary. Turn the facing to the inside, rolling the seam so it doesn't show on the right side. Press it in place.

Hand- or machine-hem the upper edge of the facing to the fabric (see pages 64–65). From the outside, the facing should be invisible.

adding a ruffle: Cut a ruffle from fabric or trim equal to 2 1/2 times the circumference of the edge it will be sewn to. Make the ruffle as wide as you want plus 1/2" (1.3 cm) for the seam allowance and 1" (2.5 cm) for the hem allowance. For circular hems, join the short ends with right sides together to form a ring. Hem the lower edge with a narrow hem (see page 65). Sew two parallel rows of basting stitches along the upper edges of the ruffle. Then, pull the threads gently to gather the ruffle.

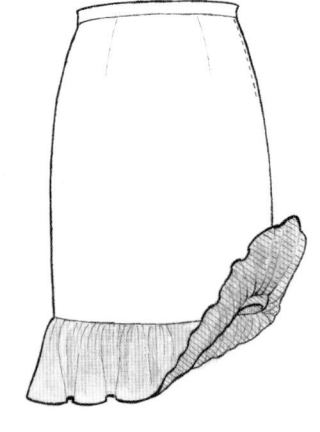

With right sides together and raw edges aligned, pin the ruffle to the bottom of the item. Stitch in place as shown. Press the seam allowances away from the ruffle, and remove the gathering threads.

If the hemline crease is difficult to press flat, try these tricks: Rub it with a clothes or lint brush. Treat it with a stain remover and clean the item. Spray it with spray starch or equal parts of white vinegar and water.

lengthening with a cuff

Cuffs are a great way to add length to clothes. You can vary the style for a sporty, casual, or tailored effect.

adding a ribbed cuff: Ready-made ribbing makes a perfect cuff for pants or sleeves. It comes with the hem edge already finished. Remove the stitching from the existing hem and press out any creases.

Measure your wrist or ankle and cut a piece of ribbed knit to fit, adding 1/2" (1.3 cm) for the seam allowance. Sew the ends together to form a ring. With right sides together, sew the unfinished edge of the rib knit to the hem edge of the item. Fold the cuff down and to the outside.

adding a woven cuff: A woven cuff is the right sort of addition to dressy or business pants or trousers. The biggest challenge is finding suitable fabric. Make sure the cuff fabric matches the garment in color, surface texture, fiber content (if possible), and weight.

1   Decide how wide you want the cuff to be. Double this measurement and add 1" (2.5 cm) for hem and seam allowances. Measure the circumference of the garment at the lower edge and add 1" (2.5 cm). Cut two pieces of fabric to these measurements.

2   With right sides together, sew the short ends to form a ring. Fold 1/2" (1.3 cm) to the wrong side of one of the cuff edges and stitch.

3   Sew the cuff and lower garment edge with right sides together, raw edges even, and with 1/2" (1.3 cm) seam allowance.

4   Fold the cuff to the inside just below the seam. Hand- or machine-stitch the finished hem edge to the garment. The stitches won't show once the cuff is formed.

5   Turn the cuff to the right side, pin and press. Tack the cuff in place at the side seams.

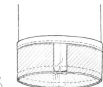
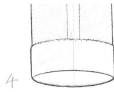
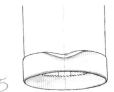

3   4   5

zipper care

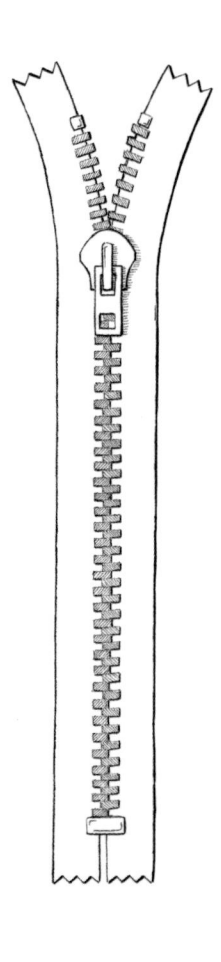

Zippers are hard-working closures. They're strong, convenient to use, and can be decorative or practically invisible. These simple tips will keep your zippers in good working order and will ensure that they have a long life.

- Keep the zipper closed when you clean or store the item.

- When opening or closing the zipper, move fabric overlaps, seam allowances, and linings away from the teeth of the zipper so the fabric doesn't get caught. Trim any loose threads in the seams.

- If fabric or threads are caught in the zipper teeth, pull the slider down to dislodge them. Never try to force the slider up.

- Brush or hose off zippers in outdoor gear, if they have collected grit, salt, or sand.

- Press the zipper area with a cool to medium-hot iron. Don't lay the iron directly over the zipper coil or teeth.

- Fix broken topstitching immediately to prevent the entire zipper installation from weakening. Attach a zipper foot and machine-stitch directly over the stitching line to connect and reinforce the still-secure stitches.

Replacing a Zipper

Most zippers are so durable they outlive the rest of the item, but they sometimes break. Try a quick fix first (see page 75–76), but if the zipper breaks a second time, you should replace it (see page 77). If the teeth or coil is damaged and the damage is not near the bottom of the zipper, the zipper probably needs to be replaced.

It isn't hard to replace a zipper, but it can be time-consuming—and in many cases it's best to work on a sewing machine. Before you take on the task yourself, call a tailor and see how much it will cost for a professional repair. Compare the expense of the repair with the cost of your free time, then decide whether the item is worth the money or the time!

repairing a zipper

It's much easier to repair a zipper than it is to replace it. Here's a list of common problems and some tips on how to fix them.

sticky zipper: Rub a candle, beeswax, or bar of soap along the teeth and then zip and unzip it a few times.

threads caught in zipper: Cut the threads with a seam ripper or sharp scissors at the point where they enter the slider. Pull out the cut threads.

fabric caught in zipper: Don't try to force the zipper open or closed. Gently pull the inside fabric (usually a lining) away from the zipper teeth or coil. Don't pull on the zipper itself.

If you can't release the fabric, carefully pry the slider or teeth off the fabric with needle-nose pliers. (The zipper might break, but it's easier to fix a zipper than to repair torn lining or fabric.)

missing teeth: If the missing tooth is near the top of the zipper, you need to replace the zipper. If a tooth is missing near the bottom of a closed-bottom zipper, move the slider above the gap.

Create a new zipper stop by stitching several straight stitches back and forth across the teeth just above the gap—or make a machine bar tack with zigzag stitches.

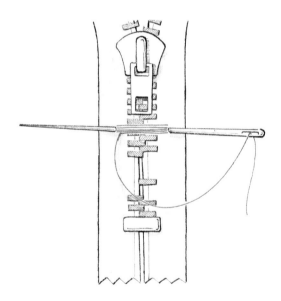

If the zipper pull is broken, you can add a decorative zipper pull that clips onto the slider. You may want to use one even if the zipper pull isn't broken!

fixing a zipper slider

The slider is the part of the zipper that opens and closes the zipper teeth or coil. Often, fixing or replacing the slider will solve your zipper problem. A pair of pliers might be all you need to return a broken zipper to good working order. Here's a list of symptoms and solutions:

slider separates from teeth or coil in the middle of the zipper: First, pry off the bottom metal stop with needle-nose pliers (or cut away the bottom 1/2" [1.3 cm] of the zipper, if that's easier). Move the slider all the way to the bottom of the zipper and off the zipper tape.

Realign the teeth and insert them back through the slider, so the zipper closes smoothly. Raise the slider. If the teeth aren't aligned and the zipper doesn't lie flat, pull the slider down and try again. Repeat until the zipper lies flat.

Close the zipper and hand-sew several straight stitches across the bottom of the zipper to create a new zipper stop. Alternatively, attach a new metal stop, as you would for a broken slider, as described below.

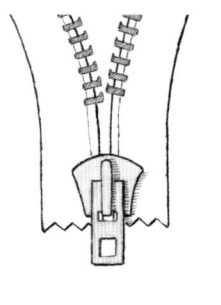

broken slider: Buy a new slider or a zipper repair kit. The kit includes a new slider and metal stops. Pry off the bottom stop with needle-nose pliers. Zip the old slider off the bottom of the zipper. Place the two zipper ends into the front two openings of the new slider. Hold the teeth together and move the slider up and down, aligning the teeth—this might take a few tries. Attach a new bottom stop by locking the ends of the metal stops around and under the zipper teeth. Or, sew the zipper closed across the bottom with several straight stitches or a zigzag bar tack (see page 75).

zipper separates in the middle or doesn't stay closed at the top: The slider is too loose. With pliers, gently squeeze the right and wrong sides of one half of the slider together. then squeeze the other half of the slider together. Apply even pressure. If this technique doesn't work, replace the slider.

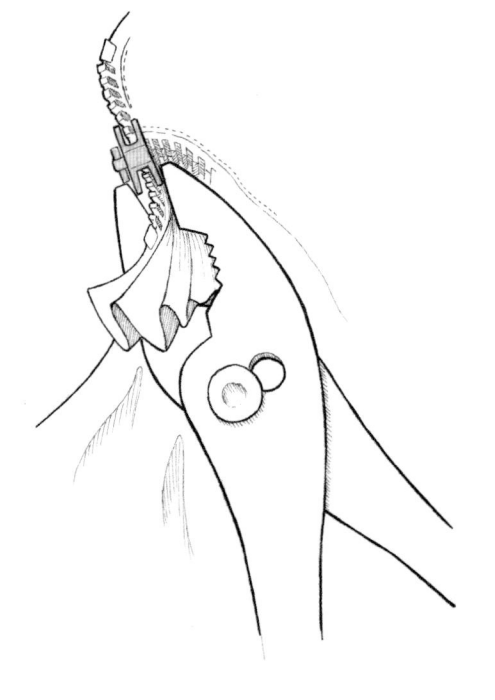

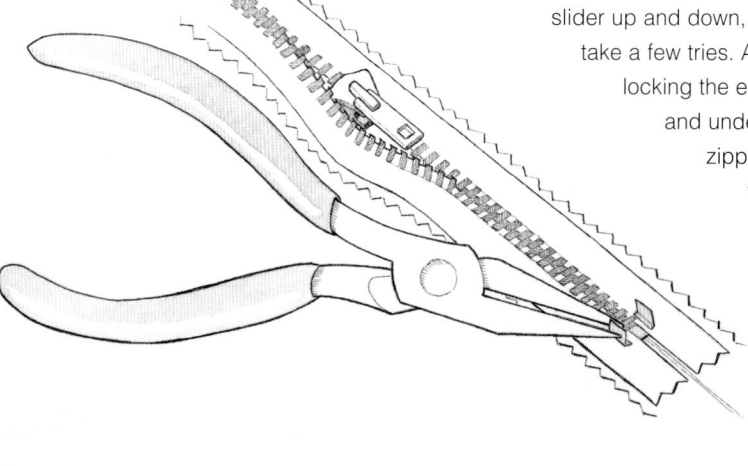

about replacing zippers

If you can't repair the zipper, you need to replace it. Prepare the new zipper by pressing the tape with a cool iron. Attach a zipper foot to your machine and adjust the needle or presser foot position so the needle is between the foot and the zipper teeth or coil.

Replacement Guidelines

- Try to buy a zipper that is the same length and color as the broken zipper. If you can't find the same length, use one that is slightly shorter—or buy a longer zipper and shorten it.

- Mark the original zipper's stitching lines with a marking pen or tailor's chalk before removing it.

- Work with a seam ripper to remove the old zipper (see page 14). If the zipper is caught in a waist-band or facing, unstitch the top edge about 1" (2.5 cm) on each side of the teeth or coil to release the zipper tape.

- Extend narrow seam allowances by stitching seam binding to the raw edges. The extensions will make it easier to install the new zipper.

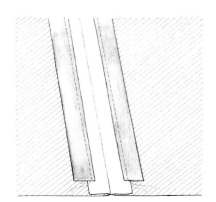

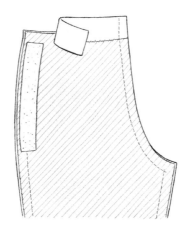

- Stabilize stretched or easily distorted fabric in the zipper area by fusing a narrow strip of interfacing to the wrong side of each seam allowance.

- Convert your machine to a free arm (check your owner's manual) to work more easily on a garment. If the zipper is in a tight or hard-to-reach spot, you might need to replace it by hand.

Shorten a Zipper

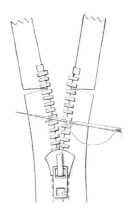

closed-bottom zippers: Close the zipper and mark the desired length (measure from the top stop). Sew a bar tack by machine or by hand (with several straight stitches) Stitch over the coil or teeth at the mark to make a new bottom stop. Trim the zipper 1/2" (1.3 cm) below the stitches.

separating zippers: Close the zipper. Measure from the bottom and mark the desired length on each side of the coil. Open the zipper and sew zigzag bar tacks at the marks on each side of the coil to form new top stops. Trim the excess zipper tape and remove the exposed coil with small, sharp scissors.

replacing a centered zipper

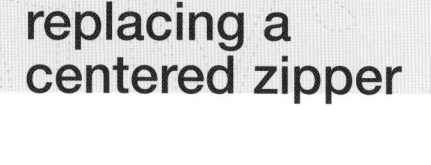

A centered zipper has two parallel rows of stitching that are each the same distance from the zipper opening in the garment. This zipper treatment is usually found in the center front or back of a dress or skirt and also in some pillow and cushion covers.

Working by Machine

Machine stitching is the best way to secure zippers that endure a lot of wear.

1. Mark the original stitching with a marking pen or tailor's chalk, using a ruler as a guide.

2. If the zipper is enclosed at the top by a facing, collar, or waistband, open the stitching at the ends of the enclosure with a seam ripper. Unstitch just enough to free the top of the zipper tape as shown in the drawing. Remove the stitches in the rest of the zipper.

3. Baste the zipper opening closed (see page 15). Press open the seam allowances.

4. With the zipper face down, center the teeth or coil over the basted seam line and position the top stop in the same location as the old top stop. Temporarily attach the zipper to the seam allowances, using a glue stick, basting tape, or basting stitches as shown in the drawing below.

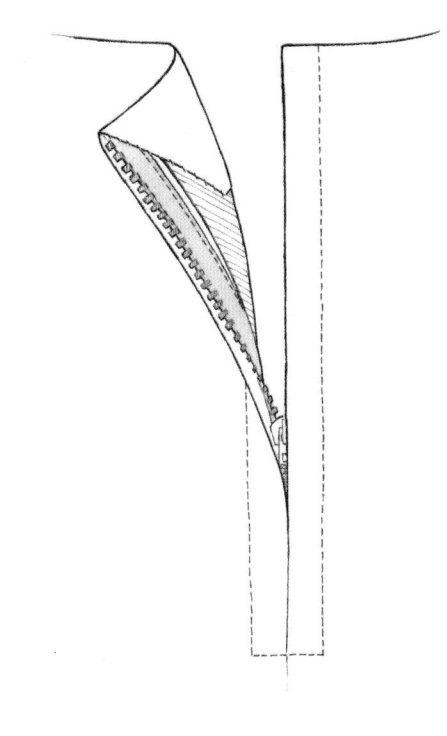

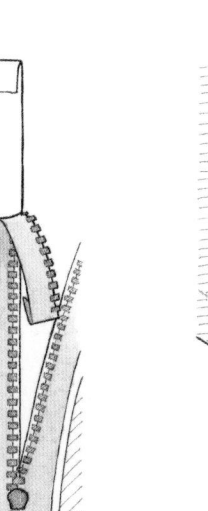

It may be hard to machine-stitch around the zipper pull. Flip it up when you position the zipper to make stitching easier.

5 Attach the zipper foot so it is on the right side of the needle. Sew directly on the marked sewing lines, starting at the bottom of the zipper. Stitch across the bottom, beginning at the seam. Pivot at the corner and stitch up the side, as shown in the drawing below.

6 Adjust the zipper foot so it is on the left side of the needle. Again, stitch across the bottom of the zipper, beginning at the seam and pivoting at the corner. Stitch up the remaining side.

7 Remove basting and markings. Press with a press cloth.

8 Stitch the facing, collar, or waistband closed, catching the top of the zipper tape in the seam, as shown in the drawing below.

Working by Hand

Long centered zippers—especially in finished garments like dresses—are hard to reach with a sewing machine. When replacing this inaccessible type of zipper, it's best to work by hand to keep the zipper and fabric from rippling.

1 Follow steps 1 through 3 for replacing the zipper by machine.

2 Starting at the bottom of the zipper, hand-sew across the bottom and up one side of the zipper. With a backstitch or a pick stitch (see page 19), stitch directly over the stitch markings as shown at right.

3 Repeat step 2 on the opposite side of the zipper. Follow steps 7 and 8 of machine application (above).

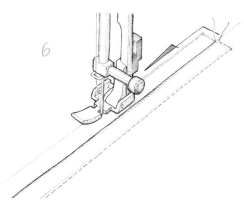

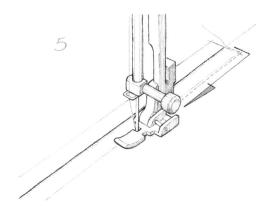

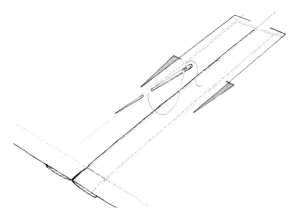

replacing a lapped zipper

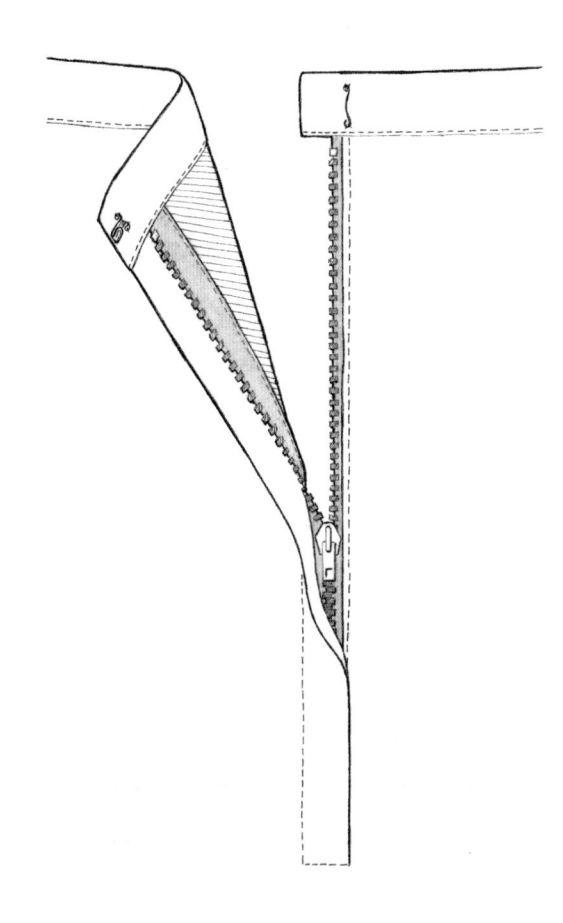

Lapped zipper applications conceal the zipper. You often find them in side seams or at the center backs of dresses, skirts, and pants. They're ideal when the color of the zipper tape, teeth, and garment fabric don't match. One row of stitching is visible on the right side of the zipper opening. The second row is stitched so close to the zipper teeth that the fabric overlap covers the zipper and the stitching. Most lapped applications use coil zippers, which are more flexible and less decorative than other zippers.

Replacing by Machine

1. Mark the previous stitching lines with a marking pen or tailor's chalk, using a ruler as a guide.

2. If the zipper is enclosed at the top with a facing, collar, or waistband, open the stitching at the ends of the enclosure just enough to free the top of the zipper tape (see the drawing on page 78). Remove the stitches in the rest of the zipper.

3. Open the replacement zipper. Position the finished, hidden edge of the garment opening on the zipper tape, close to the teeth and with right sides up as shown in the drawing at right. Temporarily hold the zipper in place with basting tape, glue stitch, or hand-basting stitches.

4. Attach a zipper foot and edge-stitch along the zipper opening, as shown in the drawing.

4

5 Close the zipper and pin the remaining finished garment edge in place, covering the zipper and the first row of stitching. Hand-baste through all layers as shown in the drawing below.

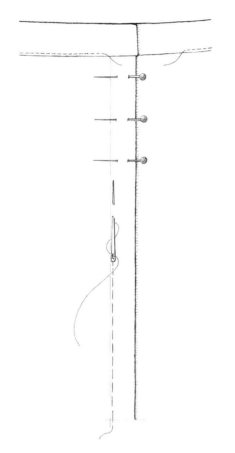

6 Move the zipper foot to the right of the needle. Starting at the seam line at the bottom of the zipper, topstitch across the bottom and up the outside edge of the zipper along the previous stitching marks.

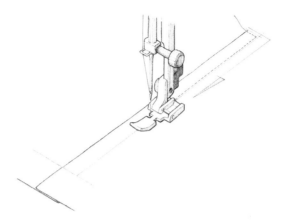

7 Remove the basting and marks. Press with a press cloth.

8 Stitch the facing, collar, or waistband closed, catching the top of the zipper tape in the seam.

Replacing by Hand

1 Follow steps 1 through 3 for replacing the zipper by machine.

2 Sew short backstitches (see page 18) to attach the first half of the zipper, as in step 4.

3 With a backstitch or a pick stitch (see page 19), sew the second half of the zipper as in step 6. These stitches will be visible on the right side of the item, so keep them neat and even. Press with a press cloth.

4 Restitch the facing, collar, or waistband, catching the top of the zipper tape in the seam.

Position 1/2" (1.3 mm)—wide household tape at the seam line to act as a topstitching guide.

replacing a fly-front zipper

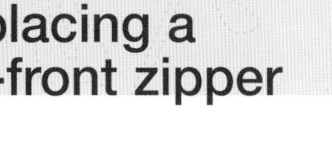

A fly-front zipper application—the style found in blue jeans—is strong and sturdy. A fly zipper has a single or double row of topstitching that curves as it nears the bottom of the zipper. This type of zipper is found only in the center front of pants or a skirt. These instructions are for a woman's garment, which laps on the left side; reverse the instructions below if your zipper laps on the right side of the zipper.

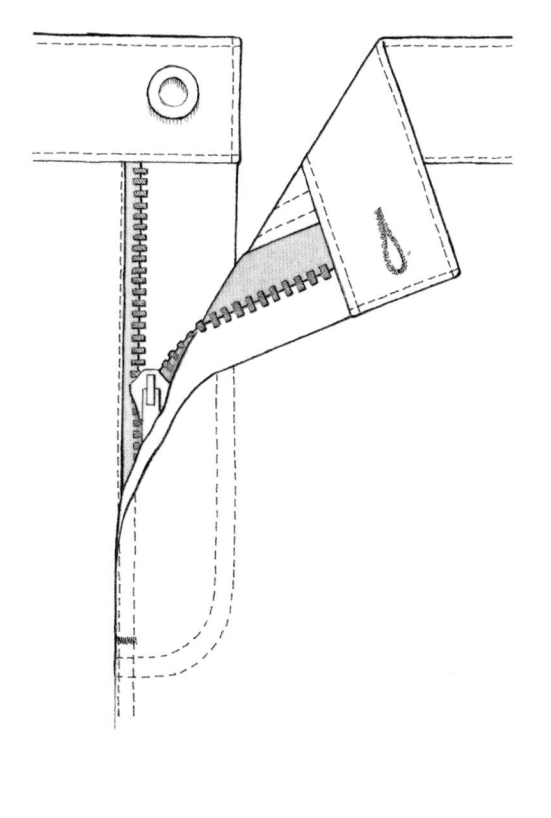

1 To avoid having to match any decorative top-stitching, remove only the stitches that hold the zipper in place (as shown in the drawing below). Cut the zipper tape at the waistband and at the lower edge to release it. With a fabric-marking pen, mark the areas where you removed stitches. If the new zipper is longer than the old one, shorten it (see page 77).

2 Fold the top edge of the side of the zipper tape to the wrong side. Slide the zipper tape into the opening you created when you removed the broken zipper. Pin the tape so the finished edge of the zipper opening is close to the teeth or coil. Hand- or machine-baste the zipper in place as shown in the drawing below.

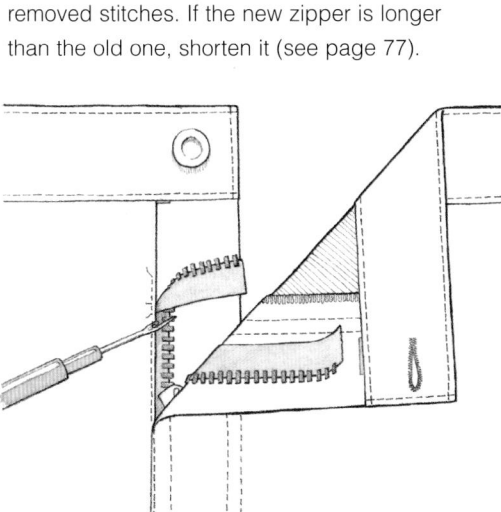

1

2

3   With the zipper foot to the left of the needle, stitch along the edge of the fabric, sewing as far down the zipper as possible. Stitch through all the layers (including the folded top of the zipper tape).

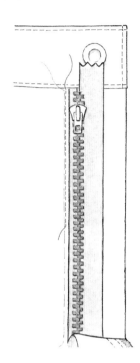

4   Close the garment and zipper. Fold the remaining top edge of the zipper tape to the front. Pin the free zipper tape in position, following the markings. Pin or hand-baste the zipper in place. Open the zipper.

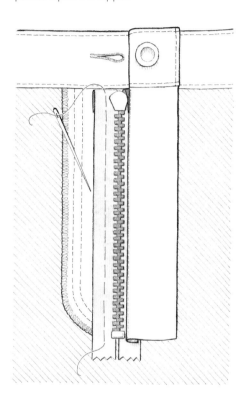

5   From the inside, backstitch the zipper tape to the fabric, sewing through only the inner layers of the fly overlap, as shown in the drawing. No stitches should show on the outside of the garment. Secure by making extra stitches at the bottom of the zipper tape. For added strength, hand-sew a few short, straight stitches across the bottom of the fly-front opening.

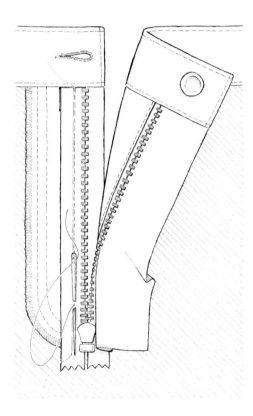

replacing a separating zipper

A separating zipper opens completely. This style is typically found in coats, jackets, outdoor gear, and sleeping bags. The zipper teeth may be concealed or exposed. You can replace a separating zipper by hand, but machine stitching is stronger. Mark the original stitching with a marking pen or tailor's chalk, using a ruler as a guide.

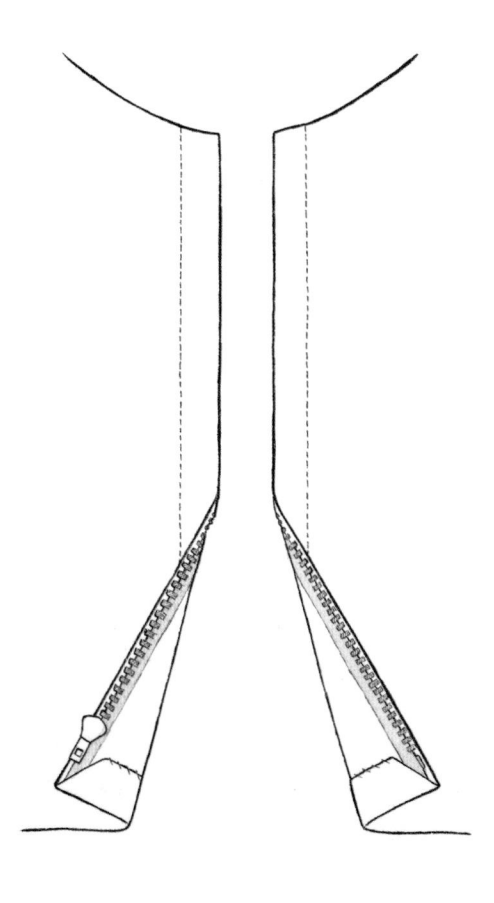

1   If the zipper is finished with a facing or collar, open the stitching just enough to free the top and bottom of the zipper tape. Then remove the stitching from the rest of the zipper.

2   If the new zipper is longer than the old one, shorten it (see page 77). Unzip the new zipper and work with one side at a time.

3   Pin the right side of the new zipper tape to the wrong side of the garment opening, with the teeth aligned along the garment edge as shown in the drawing below. Fold the top of the zipper tape under. Baste in place. If there is a facing, pin the facing in place along the zipper tape, then baste. If there is a lining, pin it out of the way.

4   Attach the zipper foot and topstitch from the right side through all layers, along the original stitching line.

5   Zip the two zipper pieces together. Pin and baste the loose half of the zipper to the other side of the garment as in step 3. Unzip the zipper and attach the remaining zipper half, repeating step 4.

6   If the garment has a lining, hand-sew it in place. With a hand-worked slipstitch, re-attach the collar or facing.

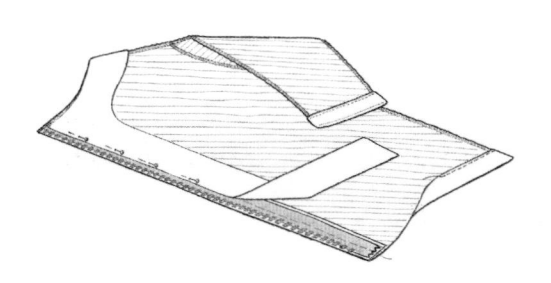

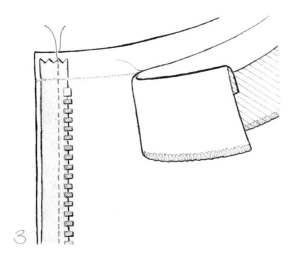

Replacing an Exposed Separating Zipper

Sometimes, the colorful, plastic zippers found in active sportswear and children's clothing are installed with the teeth exposed for a casual, sportier look.

1 Follow steps 1 and 2 for replacing a separating zipper.

2 Lay one side of the zipper face down on the right side of the fabric, with the teeth 3/4" (1.9 cm) away from the garment edge. At this point, the zipper teeth should be facing away from the opening of the garment. Pin the zipper in place. Attach the zipper foot. Stitch close to the zipper teeth as shown at lower left.

3 Fold the zipper tape to the inside of the garment, if it won't be caught in a facing or collar. Finger-press and then edge-stitch along the folded garment edge through all the layers as shown at lower right.

4 Zip the two zipper pieces together. Pin the loose half of the zipper to the other side as in step 2, aligning the upper and lower garment edges. Unzip the zipper and sew the remaining zipper half to the garment, repeating steps 2 and 3.

5 Follow step 6 for replacing a separating zipper.

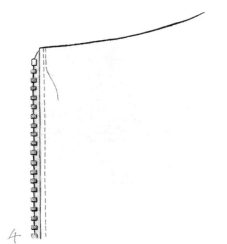

camouflaging flaws

Instead of simply mending a flaw, you might want to camouflage it in a decorative and creative way. Some fabrics are difficult to mend inconspicuously and sometimes the damage is difficult to reach by hand or machine—so a creative solution may be your only solution. Here are a few shortcuts that also add a touch of style.

- To hide a wine spot or thread snag on a cocktail dress or gown, fuse individual rhinestones in strategic places.

- Hand-sew a feather boa along the neckline of a dress to hide make-up stains or broken stitching.

- Shorten a floor-length dress to eliminate a ruined hem (see page 63). Add lace trim if you want to keep the length but hide the problem.

- Sew beads or sequins over a small, darned hole to hide the repair stitches (see page 88).

- Patch casual or children's wear with ravel-free felt and fleece appliqués in matching or contrasting colors (see page 87).

- Sew ribbon trim on old table linens to cover stains and add a splash of detail or color.

- Camouflage a mended area with fabric paint. Consider painting other areas to balance the embellishment.

- Make a ruffle or appliqué patch from a worn pillowcase. Add it to a new pillowcase that coordinates with your bedding set.

- Cut lace appliqués from scraps of lace fabric to cover anything; a neckline, a center front, a repaired zipper, the lapel of a jacket.

- Apply machine or hand embroidery stitches to cover repaired tears, snags, or stains (see page 90).

- Cover stains on upholstery by making armrest or headrest covers in beautiful, complimentary fabrics.

- If cushion covers are worn, consider remaking them by turning the original fabrics inside out (assuming the right and wrong sides are identical).

- Turn floor-length curtains into café curtains to eliminate sun-faded or frayed edges.

- Add a patch pocket in a fabulous fabric (see page 92).

decorative trim

Many beautiful trims are sold in fabric stores, and they are perfect for covering damaged fabric. Choose a trim that blends with the fabric or your garment or household item—or, for a more dramatic effect, choose one that contrasts.

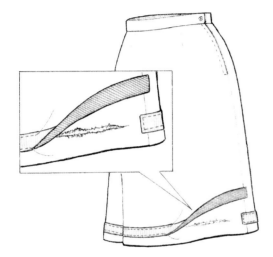

ribbon: Ribbon and other flat trims provide a quick and easy way to mend tears or holes. Baste or fuse the damage closed. Draw a placement line with a fabric-marking pen. Fuse or sew the trim directly to the damage.

bias binding: Bindings of any width enable you to easily conceal a torn fabric edge or dirty cuff edge or hem. Blanket binding, bias tape, and fold-over braid can all be machine-topstitched over any edge as shown in the drawing at the bottom left.

insertion trim: This special trim is stitched along both edges, perfect for replacing damaged fabric that is difficult to darn and too visible to patch. Position and baste the trim to form a panel over the damaged area.

Machine-stitch both edges of the insertion trim to the fabric with a narrow zigzag stitch. Cut the fabric away behind the insertion trim, close to the stitching. Apply liquid fray preventer to the cut fabric edges.

lace fabrics and trims: You can cut lace motifs and medallions from lace fabric and hand-stitch them (or zigzag-stitch by machine) in place to cover a tear or stain. Machine-topstitch lace trims along a fabric edge or hem edge to cover ravelling or abraded edges.

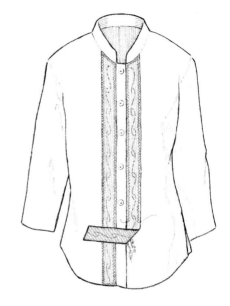

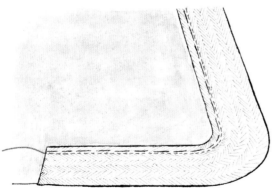

adding a
patch pocket

Cut from matching or contrasting fabric, patch pockets are great for casual wear, children's clothing, and home décor items—such as pillows, towels, tents, and tote bags. A pocket will not just cover a flaw, but add style and function to the damaged item. Make a simple, unlined patch pocket or line the pocket edge to edge with lining or self-fabric.

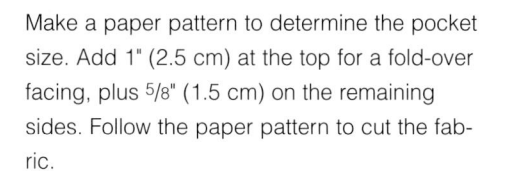

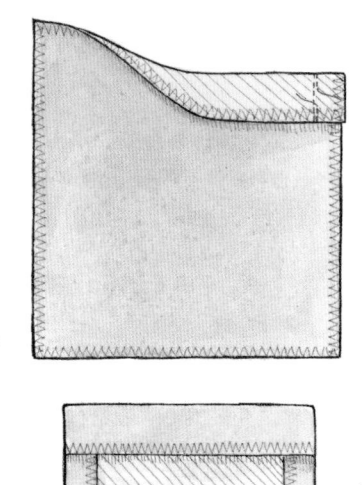

1 Make a paper pattern to determine the pocket size. Add 1" (2.5 cm) at the top for a fold-over facing, plus $5/8$" (1.5 cm) on the remaining sides. Follow the paper pattern to cut the fabric.

2 Zigzag-stitch around the edges of the pocket.

3 Fold the 1" (2.5 cm) facing to the right side. Allowing a $5/8$" (1.5 cm) seam allowance, stitch the facing in place along the pocket sides. Trim the upper corners diagonally.

Turn the facing back to the pocket's wrong side. Press.

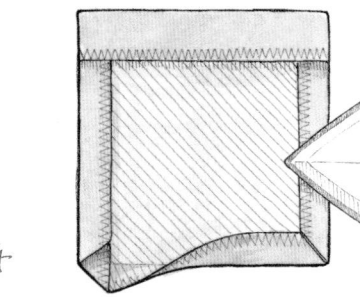

4 Press under the $5/8$" (1.5 cm) allowances on the remaining sides. Miter the corners.

5 Topstitch the pocket facing in place as shown at left.

6 Position the pocket on top of the damaged area and edge-stitch it in place. Backstitch or sew a small reinforcing triangle at each top corner for extra strength.

adding a pocket flap

A pocket flap usually covers the tailored pockets of suit coats and jackets. If you need to conceal a hole or stain, however, you can make a false pocket flap. A pocket flap looks best when it's lined with lining or fashion fabric. Mend any tears before covering them with flaps.

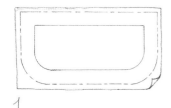

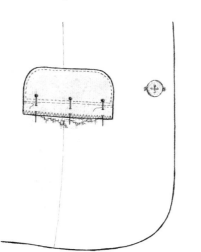

1 Determine the flap size and shape by cutting a piece of paper and placing it over the damaged fabric. Add 5/8" (1.5 cm) all around for seam allowance.

Follow the paper pattern to cut two pieces of fabric for each flap, one of fashion fabric and the other of lining.

2 Sew the pieces with right sides together, leaving the top edge open and backstitching at the upper corners. Trim the seam allowances and clip corners as needed. Turn the flap right side out and press.

3 Edge-stitch around the sides and bottom of the flap if desired to match the detailing of the garment. Zigzag-stitch the top edges together.

4 Press the top 1/2" (1.3 cm) of the flap under. Position the flap over the damaged area. Pin only the folded upper edge to the garment. Open the flap. Stitch 1/2" (1.3 cm) from the top edge, along the pressed fold line.

5 Fold the flap back over the stitching. Machine-topstitch along the upper fold to hold the flap in place.

refolding pleats

There are so many ways to hide fabric flaws, you might never have to throw anything away! If you can't mend or clean something so that the repair is entirely invisible, you can sometimes conceal the telltale signs by refolding the pleats in the opposite direction. Mend holes or tears first, so they don't get larger.

box pleats: To conceal a hole, tear, or stain, simply convert a box pleat to an inverted pleat—or vice versa. Remove the stitching that holds the pleat in place. Refold the pleat in reverse to hide the fabric flaw. Press to set the new folds and restitch, as shown in the drawing below. If the garment has more than one pleat, reverse the other pleats, too.

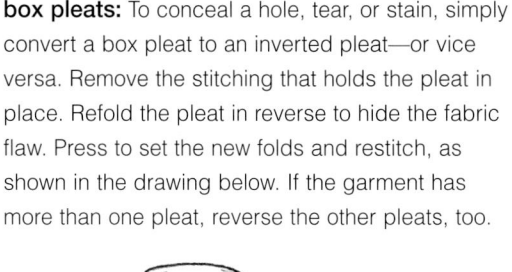

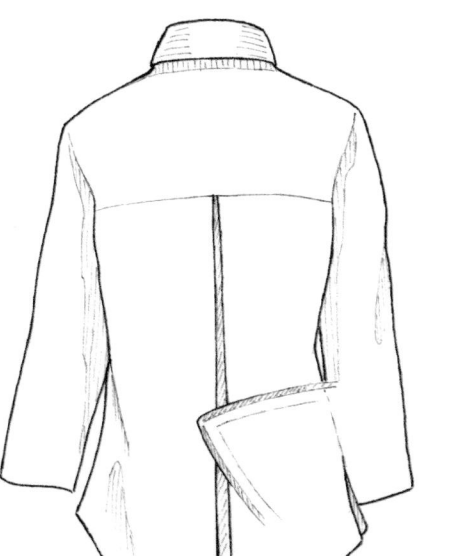

knife pleats: Knife pleats are a series of pleats that are all folded in the same direction. You find them most often on skirts. To hide damage on the garment, remove the waistband and refold the pleats in the opposite direction as shown in the drawing below at right. Press the new pleats to set them. Then replace the waistband.

mini makeovers

With creative mending, repairing, and decorating, just think about how you can transform once-loved but out-of-date clothes. Instead of staring at a closet full of clothes that don't inspire you, you can step out in style! Here are a few suggestions to get you started.

- Dye the garment. This solution works best for light-colored fabrics.
- Fix a dirty hemline by covering it with trim, shortening the item, or using your overlock machine to create a lettuce edge finish.
- Add or remove trim, whichever suits your taste.
- Narrow the garment's silhouette by tapering the skirt, legs, or sleeves.
- Add volume and flow to skirts by inserting fabric panels in seams.
- Open a seam up from the hem to create a slit or vent in skirts or pants.
- Add a layer of organza under the skirt or as an overskirt.
- Remove sleeves from tops or dresses and add trim around the armholes—or create straps with purchased trim. Convert a jacket into a vest.
- Lower the neckline.
- Reshape the neckline.
- Fuse iron-on rhinestones for extra sparkle.
- Shorten the garment dramatically. Turn a dress into a tunic, or a jacket into a cropped bolero.
- Update closures with decorative buttons, hooks, zipper pulls, etc.
- Cut off pants at hip level and add fabric bands or ruffles to make a skirt.

If you love wearing one-of-a-kind garments, shop at thrift stores for inexpensive garments, then restyle them to create your own look.

mending lace

Lace appears fragile and delicate, but it's simple to mend. The repair stitches disappear into the intricate pattern of the lace.

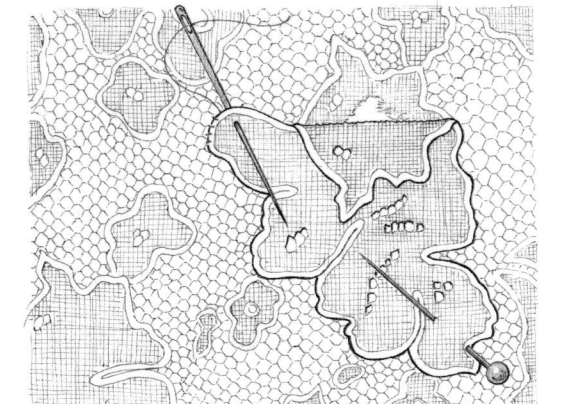

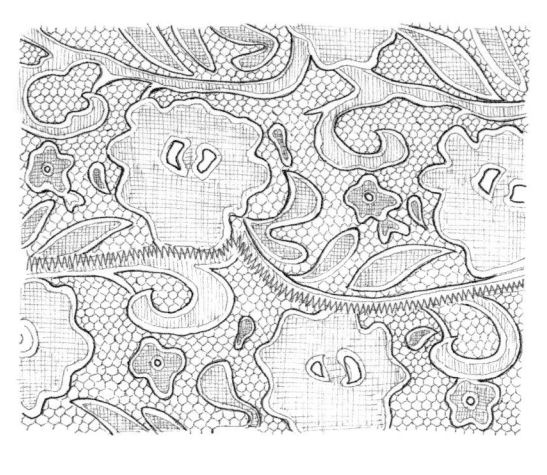

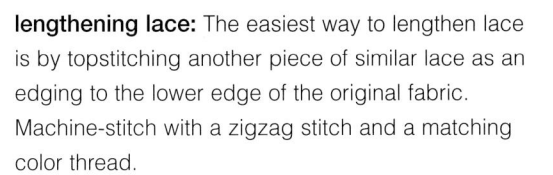
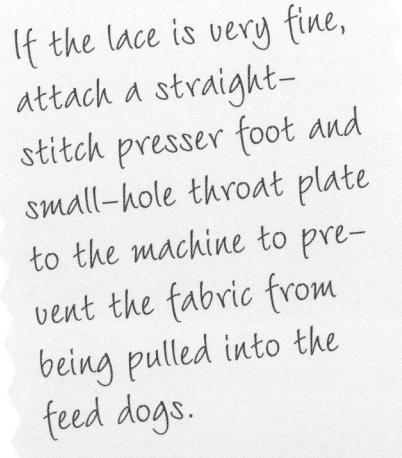

mending a hole: To repair a section of lace, cut a similar or similar size motif from a lace that is the same color, texture, and density. Center the motif over the hole and slipstitch around the edges. Work with a single strand of matching thread—silk thread is best, if you have it. You can also repair holes by machine with small zigzag stitches.

mending a tear: Bring together the edges of the tear, overlapping them slightly. Hand-baste them together. Machine-zigzag over the edges with thread of matching color.

shortening lace: If the lace has a finished or shaped edging that you don't want to fold under, mark a straight line across the top of the edging. Cut along the line. Shorten the item (see page 69) to the desired length.

Zigzag-stitch or hand-sew the section you removed onto the shortened lower edge with matching thread. You can also shorten the item from the waist (see page 69). If the original hem was folded and stitched, shorten it using the same method.

lengthening lace: The easiest way to lengthen lace is by topstitching another piece of similar lace as an edging to the lower edge of the original fabric. Machine-stitch with a zigzag stitch and a matching color thread.

If the lace is very fine, attach a straight-stitch presser foot and small-hole throat plate to the machine to prevent the fabric from being pulled into the feed dogs.

mending leather and suede

It's a challenge to make inconspicuous repairs in leather and suede. These techniques work well, however, for both real and synthetic leather and suede. Synthetic leather and suede are nonwoven so they don't fray. Do not use fusibles on these fabrics.

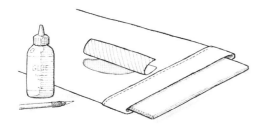 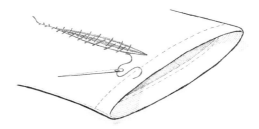 

patching a hole: Neaten the edges of the hole with a razor blade, cutting carefully on a cutting mat. Place a piece of paper under the hole and trace the opening to create a paper template. Cut a patch of matching leather to the same size as the template. Insert the leather patch into the hole.

Cut a piece of fabric backing from medium-weight, firm cotton or linen or from lightweight canvas. The piece should be about 1" (2.5 cm) larger all around than the patch.

With the wrong side up, apply leather adhesive or strong fabric glue to the wrong side of the fabric backing. Center it over the wrong side of the patch and finger-press it in place. Put a heavy weight on the patch and let the adhesive set for at least an hour.

mending a tear: Abut the edges of the tear so their surfaces are flush. If the tear is in a location that is subject to strain, hand-sew the wrong side closed with a widely spaced slanting stitch. Work with a heavy needle and polyester thread.

If necessary, apply adhesive to a cotton or canvas backing and apply the backing to the wrong side of the leather, covering the tear, as described above.

repairing a snag: If you catch your favorite leather jacket on a sharp object and it tears slightly, don't worry. Repair the surface tear by carefully applying a small dab of clear nail polish under the snag. Firmly but gently press the mended area

shortening leather: Cut the leather to the length desired, adding 1/2" (1.3 cm) for hem allowance. Fold the allowance to the wrong side, then topstitch or glue it in place. To set the new hemline, pound the folded hem edge with a rubber mallet or cloth-covered hammer.

lengthening leather: You can't let down a hem in leather. The easiest option for lengthening is to add a decorative trim to the lower edge of the garment.

Stitch with a longer-than-usual stitch (5—8 stitches per inch [2.5 cm]). Remember, needle holes are permanent in leather.

mending pile fabrics

Pile fabrics are also referred to as fabrics "with nap"—a fabric whose surface fibers have an obvious direction. Pile fabrics include favorites such as terrycloth, velvet, corduroy, sweatshirt fleece, wool flannel, suede cloth, and fake fur.

- Set the sewing machine for about 5 to 8 stitches per inch (2.5 cm).
- Stitch a straight seam on most napped fabrics. For fabrics with a stretch knit backing, use a narrow zigzag stitch.
- Press the fabric on the wrong side, with the pile face down on a terrycloth towel or on a piece of self-fabric with the pile side up.
- Reduce bulk by trimming pile from the seam allowance.
- Zigzag all the raw edges of medium- to heavyweight fabrics.
- Clean-finish the seam allowances of lightweight fabrics with a zigzag stitch or fold the edge to the wrong side and stitch it in place.

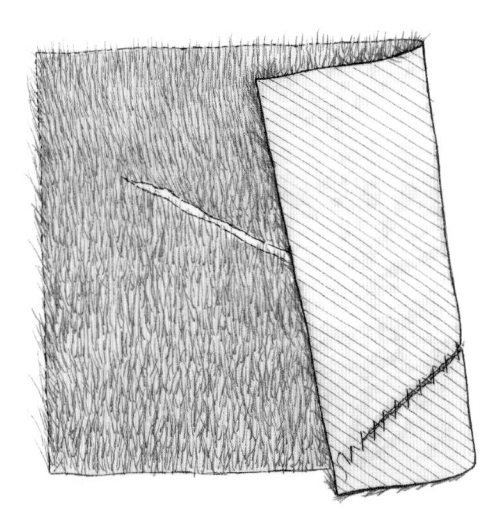

Any patches you apply to a pile fabric need to have fibers that run in the same direction as the original fabric. Work all the mending on the wrong side, as shown, and brush the pile to cover the mending. If you need to patch fake fur, try the same patching technique that you would use for leather (page 97).

Saving Crushed Velvet

If a velvet fabric has been crushed, you can turn the crush marks into a design feature by adding embossed motifs around and over them. Place the velvet face down over a rubber stamp. Spray the wrong side with water. With a dry iron, press over the stamp for 20 to 30 seconds (or until the water is dry). Lift the iron straight up and peel the fabric off the stamp.

mending stretch knits

Machine-knit fabrics are easy to sew, but not as easy to mend. Lightweight, smooth-surfaced knits, like jersey or interlock, are often difficult to darn or patch invisibly. Consider these techniques—or a decorative repair for your more casual garments and items.

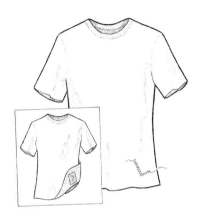

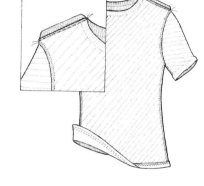

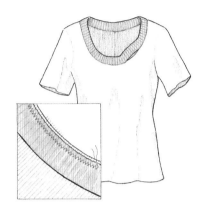

mending a hole or tear: Fuse a patch of interfacing with moderate stretch to the wrong side over the hole or tear. On the right side, machine-zigzag over the tear to reinforce the fusible patch.

reshaping: Often, a trip through the washer and dryer brings a stretched-out knit back to shape. You can also lay the garment on an ironing board and steam-press it into the desired shape by holding the steam iron above it slightly to dampen the fibers.

stabilizing seams: Some seams—usually shoulder, neckline, and waist seams—need to be stabilized so they don't stretch. To do so, sew a piece of twill tape or ribbon to the seam allowance.

shortening: Hem knits with a twin needle or a straight stretch stitch as shown at center, above. Match the number of rows of stitching to those used elsewhere on the garment.

repairing ribbed trim: Many knit shirts have a band of ribbed trim at the neckline, hem, armholes, or sleeve hems. Neckline seams are narrow and often come unstitched.

Turn the garment inside out and pin the edges of the opening together. Machine-zigzag the two edges together, close to the raw edges.

washing and drying

If you'd like to water-proof a garment, check at your local fabric or outdoor gear store for a wash-in or spray-on product, such as Nikwax.

When it comes to mending and repairing, you can fix a lot of problems before they even begin with regular laundering and cleaning of your clothing, upholstery, and carpet.

Machine-washing

- Read all care labels, pretreat stains (see page 105) and repair tears or loose trim.

- Zip zippers, empty pockets, unroll cuffs, and turn colored items inside out.

- Wash brightly colored, new items alone for the first time to make sure the dye doesn't run.

- Sort clothing and other items into separate wash loads by color, fabric weight (heavy jeans should be separated from delicate items), lint production, and whether they are heavily soiled.

- Set the washing machine to the regular cycle for sturdy fabrics and very dirty clothing, to the permanent press cycle for most laundry loads, and to the delicate cycle for lightweight and delicate items.

- Wash most laundry in warm water. Hot water is suitable for white clothing or very dirty, colorfast clothes. Bright colors and delicate fabrics are best suited to cold-water wash.

- Select a washing time of 6 to 8 minutes for an adequate washing time.

- Add the recommended amount of detergent to the washing machine. Extra detergent is actually harmful to many fabrics.

- Start the water; add detergent; add the clothes. Fill the washing machine 3/4 full so the clothes have room to move around.

Machine-drying

- Remove delicate items while they are still damp and hang them or lay them flat to dry.

- Opt for the air-fluff cycle, which circulates unheated air to plump pillows and refresh clothes that have been packed away.

- Do not machine-dry clothes or home décor items that may shrink.

- Keep dryer loads small. Clothes dry faster if they can circulate.

- Don't dry heavy clothes with delicate ones, or the delicate items will overheat.

- Do not put wool or silk garments into the dryer.

- Remove the lint from the dryer every time you use it. A lint-filled filter is a fire hazard and uses more energy than a clean filter.

- Wash the filter with soap and water periodically.

- Don't machine-dry stained items. The heat will permanently set the stain. Instead, hang the item to dry, then retreat the stain.

Hand-Washing and Hang Drying

- Hand-wash delicate items, specialty fabrics, wool sweaters, stained items, items with specialty trims, and any item you aren't sure of the best way to clean.

- Pretreat stains.

- Fill a basin or sink with cool water and mild detergent. Put the clothing in the basin and let it set for a few minutes. Gently work the suds through the fibers. Do not rub the fabric layers together. Rinse with cool water several times. Do not wring out the water. Gently squeeze the item or roll it in a clean towel.

- Lay knits or other stretchy items flat on an absorbent towel to dry. Hang wovens and nonstretch items on a hanger in the bathroom or laundry room to dry. Straighten and close garments so they maintain their shape as they dry.

Dry Cleaning

- Dry cleaning relies on special solvents and a minimal amount of water.

- Some items can be hand-washed even when the care label indicates to dry-clean. If in doubt, take the item to the dry cleaner.

- Items that should be dry-cleaned include: delicate fabrics like silk, chiffon, fur, and some wools, items that shrink easily, and tailored items.

- Empty pockets and remove specialty buttons or trims.

- Point out any stains to the dry cleaner.

If a velveteen or corduroy fabric becomes flat or matted, put it in the dryer with a damp towel to "raise" the nap.

fixing ironing accidents

It doesn't matter how careful you are, everyone has ironing accidents. Often the damage is reversible—especially if you get to it right away.

for crushed pile: Pile fabrics can become crushed in a crowded closet or along crease lines if they're stored folded. Machine-wash and machine-dry the damaged item right away.

Throw a damp towel in the dryer with it, and the moisture will help revive the pile.

You can also hang the item in a steamy bathroom while the shower is running. Brush the area with a stiff-bristled clothes brush to lift the pile.

for a scorch mark: Place the damaged fabric on a dry towel. Blot it with diluted hydrogen peroxide and let it set. Rinse with clear water. Move the treated area to a dry area of the towel.

If the scorch mark is still visible, apply diluted detergent and water. Alternate the cleaning solutions, dabbing them gently on the burn marks.

for pressing marks: steam the area really well. Gently rub the pressing marks with a soft cloth or your fingers. If the fabric is machine washable, spray it with water from a spray bottle and rub gently.

for iron drips or water spots: place an absorbent cloth over the water spot, and as long as the item is machine washable, spray it with a fine mist of water from a spray bottle. Press, the extra moisture should disperse the water ring.

Don't press over a stained area, or you will permanently set the stain.

storing garments

Whether you are storing garments for a season or for a longer time, make sure they are clean and stain-free before you put them away. It's okay to wash and dry them by machine, but don't use soap, chlorine bleach, starch, or fabric softeners, which can damage or discolor fibers over time, or attract insects. Dry-clean any items that are specified as "dry clean only."

Do not store clothes in plastic bags or airtight containers that restrict the flow of air around the garments. Store everything in a well-ventilated area that is free of moisture, extreme temperature variations, and sunlight. So, storage in the attic, basement, or garage is not ideal. Try to find a storage area in your living area. Store the items flat or on padded or rounded hangers.

When you take the garments out of storage, put them in the dryer (if their care requirements allow) on the air-fluff setting to eliminate wrinkles.

Don't use wire hangers. They can rust, stain or snag the fabric. Remove any pins before storing garments — they can rust, stain, and snag, too.

flat storage *(for sweaters, knits and stretchy fabrics, delicate and fragile fabrics):* Fold wool sweaters and store them flat. Try to avoid creasing the items by layering them with acid-free tissue paper. Place the heaviest and bulkiest items on the bottom.

Use an acid-free box for long-term flat storage and a cedar chest for woolen items. Store heavily embellished garments, such as beaded gowns, flat. Stuff them with acid-free tissue paper to prevent crushing.

flat storage *(for heirloom-quality items):* To protect the fibers, store wedding dresses, holiday garments, and heirloom baby clothes flat. Clean the items first, then wrap them in buffered acid-free paper (for cotton and linen) or non-buffered acid-free paper (for silk and wool).

Stuff the sleeves, bodices, and upper part of skirts with tissue paper to avoid creasing the garment. Place the garment in an acid-free box, lined with a white sheet or muslin. Be sure there is enough room in the box that the garment isn't crushed.

hanging storage *(for jackets, suits, sheer blouses, dresses, tailored garments, window treatments, and outerwear):* Clean the items and remove any plastic dry-cleaning bags. Hang the garments or other items on padded, shaped hangers (in or out of clothes bags) in a well-ventilated closet. Allow space for air to circulate between garments. Button, zip, or otherwise fasten the garment so it holds its shape while stored.

fabric-cleaning products

There are many fabric-cleaning and stain-removal products on the market—but all you need are a few basics. These basic cleaning products are appropriate for clothes, carpets, and upholstery. Never mix stain-removal products—when combined, bleach and ammonia produce toxic fumes. Always store cleaning products safely out of the reach of young children.

laundry detergent: Detergent is available in liquid or powder form. Liquid detergent disperses better than powder and also works for on-the-spot stain removal (although detergents that contain fabric softener are not as effective at stain removal). Only use the amount recommended by the manufacturer.

enzyme cleaners and detergents: These products are great for removing food stains. They also remove surface fibers that cause pilling. Check the labels of your cleaning products, however, because some already contain enzymes.

liquid dishwashing detergent: Diluted with water, dishwashing liquid is remarkably versatile. Store it in a spray bottle and keep it on hand for quick stain removal on clothing, upholstery, and carpets.

bleach: Available in both chlorine and nonchlorine varieties, bleach helps to whiten whites and remove stains. But it's too harsh for everyday use and fades and wears out fabrics when overused. If you soak a stain in diluted bleach, it should come out in fifteen minutes. If it doesn't, nothing will get that stain out!

- Nonchlorine bleach is gentler than chlorine bleach and can be used on most fabrics.

- Chlorine bleach is very strong and should be used sparingly, but does a great job whitening whites and removing stains on white items. Do not use it on acrylic, silk, spandex, linen, or wool fabrics.

- Hydrogen peroxide is a mild bleach. When it's diluted with water you can use it on silk and wool.

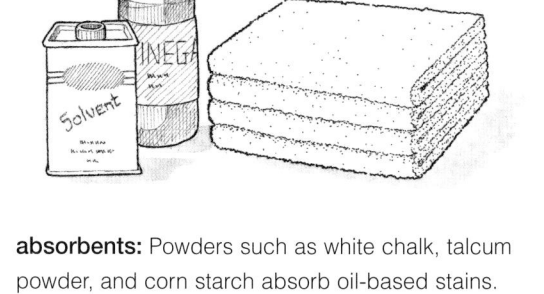

absorbents: Powders such as white chalk, talcum powder, and corn starch absorb oil-based stains. Sprinkle one on the stain, let it set, and then brush off the powder.

prewash treatments: These laundry aids are available in gels, squeeze bottles, pump and aerosol sprays, and stick form. They enable you to pretreat a stain as soon as you notice it.

white distilled vinegar: Add vinegar to laundry rinse water to remove excess detergent and make clothes softer and fresher. It also reduces static electricity and odors. White vinegar removes fruit, wine, coffee, and tea stains. Don't use it on cotton, silk, acetate, or linen fabrics.

dry-cleaning solvents: For spot-cleaning dry-clean-only items, look for these solvents. The fumes are strong, so only use these products outdoors or in a well-ventilated area.

how to treat a stain

The sooner you attack the stain, the less time it has to react with the fabric fibers. Sunlight, hot water, heat, and time make it harder to remove stains. Always refer to the care label in the garment before trying any cleaning product or method.

1   Blot excess liquid with a clean towel or rag.

2   Gently scrape solids (mud, chewy candy, etc.) off the surface of fabric with a dull knife.

3   Sprinkle an absorbent powder on greasy spills (see page 104). Rinse nongreasy spills with cool water or club soda.

4   Before pretreating stains, test the cleaning product on a hidden area to be sure it won't affect the color. Choose from among the cleaning agents on page 104 to treat the stain.

5   Apply the cleaning agent. Do not rub a stained area. Rubbing can spread the stain and damage the fibers. Dab to blot, with a gentle touch. Rinse the item.

6   Let the item air-dry and then check to see that all traces of the stain are gone. If not, apply the cleaning agent again. Rinse and let air-dry. (Never put a stained item in the dryer or on a radiator—the heat might set the stain.)

7   When all traces of the stain are gone, machine-wash or dry-clean as usual.

Avoid washing stains with bar soap—this type of soap can sometimes set stains.

caring for carpets and upholstery

Routine cleaning is essential for maintaining upholstery fabrics and carpets—just as it is for clothing. Keep dirt and dust from accumulating by vacuuming your carpet once a week and your upholstery once a month. Rotate furniture cushions often and vacuum them, using your vacuum cleaner's upholstery nozzle and crevice tool.

Spot-Cleaning Carpets and Upholstery

If you get a spill on your upholstery or carpet, blot, don't rub, it immediately and remove any solid particles. Treat the stain as soon as you can, following the steps below. The longer you wait, the more likely it is that the stain will set permanently.

1 Select a cleaning solution. You may use a dry-cleaning solvent or pretreatment spot remover, diluted dish detergent, or mix a solution of half vinegar and half water. Test the cleaning solution in an inconspicuous area first to double-check that it doesn't damage the fabric or alter its color.

2 If the stained fabric or rug can be moved, lay it, face down, over a clean, absorbent white towel or rag, which will absorb the stain. Otherwise—for upholstered furniture or wall-to-wall carpet—work from the right side.

3 Dampen a towel with the cleaning solution you've chosen. Gently dab the stain from the wrong side, if possible, or from the right side. With small, light strokes, feather the outer edges of the stain to avoid creating a visible outline around the stained area.

4 Move the underlying towel, if present, so that a clean area is under the stain. This will help draw more of the stain out of the fabric. Repeat until the stain is gone.

5 Launder or dry-clean the item, if possible, to remove traces of the solvent.

Vacuum carpets along the wall carefully. Dust and dirt collect there and create dingy shadows.

stain removal chart

Always attend to stains as quickly as possible. Some stains require a combination of treatments. Treat for an oil or grease stain first, and then any other causes of the stain. This stain-removal chart is for washable fabrics only.

unknown stains: If you don't know the source of the stain, fill a small squirt bottle with cool water and a teaspoon of liquid hand dishwashing soap. Squirt the stain liberally and let it sit. Rinse with cool water. If this doesn't work, soak it in a mixture of one part white vinegar and two parts cool water.

fruit and beverage stains *(beer, wine, cologne, soft drinks, coffee, tea, berries):* Soak for 15 minutes in one quart of lukewarm water, one half teaspoon liquid dishwashing detergent and one tablespoon white vinegar. Rinse.

greasy stains *(butter, margarine, cooking oil, lotions, mayonnaise, salad dressing):* Sprinkle with cornstarch, cornmeal, or powder and let it set to absorb the grease. Brush it off after 15 to 30 minutes. Apply pretreatment stain remover. Spray types work better on greasy stains. Let it sit for a few minutes and then launder as soon as possible.

protein stains *(blood, eggs, vomit, milk products):* Scrape off the cause of the stain. Soak in cold water with one-half teaspoon liquid hand dishwashing detergent for fifteen minutes, rinse. If stain persists, soak in enzyme product and then launder. If it's necessary and safe for the fabric, wash with chlorine bleach.

stains from dyes *(cherry, blueberries, fabric dye bleeding, felt-tip markers, grass, artificial food colors):* These stains are challenging. Pretreat and then soak the stained item in water and nonchlorine bleach. If you can still see the stain, and the fabric is suitable, wash the entire item with chlorine bleach.

Stain Removal Chart

Stain	Treatment
Ballpoint Ink	Rub gently with a pen eraser. Dry cleaning solvent, rubbing alcohol, glycerin, or hairspray may also remove ink. If not, wet the stain and sponge it with mild detergent and a few drops of vinegar. Let it sit for 30 minutes. Rinse and wash as usual, hang to dry.
Blood	If the stain is fresh, soak it in cold water. Dab on diluted ammonia. Soak a dry blood stain in cold salt water for several hours, then rinse. If the stain persists, apply an enzyme prewash product and then a non-chlorine bleach.
Chocolate	Treat the spot with diluted hand dishwashing detergent or an enzyme detergent and water. Let it sit for 30 minutes, then rinse.

Stain Removal Chart

Stain	Treatment
Grass	Apply a paste of dishwasher detergent and water or pre-treatment product. Let it sit for 30 minutes. Rinse with cool water. Remove any remaining stain with diluted ammonia or nonchlorine bleach. Rinse and wash with an enzyme detergent in regular cycle with cool water. Don't machine dry until the stain is completely removed.
Lipstick	Scrape off the excess with a dull knife or the edge of a spoon. Apply a dry-cleaning solvent, let it dry, then brush it off. Wash with gentle detergent and cool water. If stain persists, dab with diluted ammonia. Rinse with cool water. If necessary and fabric allows, wash with diluted chlorine bleach.
Mildew	Apply a pretreatment product and wash with hottest water appropriate for the fabric. Spot treat with hydrogen peroxide. If mildew has formed on upholstery, sponge surface with liquid hand dishwashing detergent and minimal water. Dry in the sun if possible.
Mud	Let the mud dry, and shake or scrape off excess. Apply pretreatment product or diluted dishwashing detergent and soak. Wash with enzyme detergent.
Perspiration	Apply pretreatment product. Launder with enzyme detergent in hottest water recommended for the fabric. If stain persists, wash with oxygen bleach or vinegar.
Rust	The best remedy is a rust removal product. Or, sprinkle salt over the area and then spray it with lemon juice. Put it in the sun to dry, but make sure the lemon juice doesn't bleach the fabric by testing it on the wrong side first.
Urine	Rinse in cold water and wash in the regular cycle. To remove urine stains from mattresses, sponge the stain with a rag soaked with water and detergent or water and vinegar. Allow to air-dry.
Water Spots	Dampen the entire item with water and air dry. Or, hold the stain over the steam from a boiling kettle. Launder as usual.
Wax	Put the item in the freezer for 20 minutes to harden the wax. Scrape off the wax with a dull knife. Stretch the stained area over a bowl and pour boiling water over it to melt the remaining wax.
Wine, Red	Cover the stain with salt. Then stretch the stained area over a bowl and pour boiling water over it. If the stain persists, spray it with diluted white vinegar, or apply hydrogen peroxide.
Wine, White	A white wine stain can turn brown. Flush the area with cold water and liquid dishwashing detergent, or treat it with enzyme detergent and wash it in the regular cycle.

index